The Gardens of LOUISIANA

The Gardens
of LOUISIANA

PLACES OF WORK AND WONDER

Photographs by A. J. MEEK

Text by SUZANNE TURNER

LOUISIANA STATE UNIVERSITY PRESS

BATON ROUGE AND LONDON

Copyright © 1997 by Louisiana State University Press
Manufactured in Hong Kong
First printing
06 05 04 03 02 01 00 99 98 97   5 4 3 2 1

Designer: Laura Roubique Gleason
Typeface: Adobe Garamond
Printer and binder: C & C Offset Printing Company

LIBRARY OF CONGRESS CATALOGING-IN-PUBLICATION DATA
Meek, A. J.
    The gardens of Louisiana : places of work and wonder / photographs by
A. J. Meek ; text by Suzanne Turner.
            p.   cm.
    Includes bibliographical references and index.
    ISBN 0-8071-2107-x (cloth : alk. paper)
    1. Gardens of Louisiana.   2. Gardens—Louisiana—Pictorial works.
I. Turner, Suzanne, date.   II. Title.
SB466.U65L685   1997
536' .09763—dc21   96-53547
                                                              CIP

Contents

Author's Preface

Gardens live such a fleeting existence that the urge to capture them and make them timeless—through photography, literature, painting—seems universal. In Harnett Kane's *Plantation Parade,* the first two chapters, "Louis XIV of Louisiana" and "Disenchanted Gardens," tell the story of Valcour Aime, of St. James Parish, a planter who, as one of the most successful growers of sugarcane between 1820 and 1860, built for himself and his family not only an economic empire but a garden grand enough to become known as Le Petit Versailles. The garden Aime and his slaves built as a playground for his grandchildren and as a horticultural experiment survives today as only a jungle of trees and undergrowth, with remnants of a fortress, a mound, a cascade, a rivulet, and bridges. Even overgrown, however, it stands in testament to the intimate connections between people and their gardens that have distinguished Louisiana gardens from the earliest days of settlement.

Gardens have always been prominent in the story of Louisiana. Travelers' accounts from the eighteenth century often begin with remarks on the exotic, lush natural forest or the gardens of settlers. The oldest maps of the city of New Orleans show elaborately geometric parterre gardens as distinctly as they do the few dwellings. Whether these gardens existed as mapped or were purely the car-tographers' conception of what a prospering frontier settlement ought to look like, they gave expression to the relationship between architecture and landscape in the French colony. The success of colonization depended on the landscape. It was the location of that landscape—its proximity by way of the Mississippi to the markets of the world—and its long and moderate growing season that made Louisiana suitable as one of the first areas on the continent with a permanent European presence. The Europeans were, of course, not the first to take advantage of the rich resources of the Louisiana landscape. Native Americans had inhabited the region for centuries, relying upon the abundant game, shellfish, and native plants, and benefiting from the climate and soil fertility. They passed on the results of their garden experiments to the Europeans, and with that, an initial step had been taken toward the great mélange of cultures of the place.

Collectively, the gardens of Louisiana are perhaps the most diverse and arresting of any state's in the nation. Although superlatives may make little difference to the garden lover or the student of garden history, it is important to appreciate that this book illuminates a key component of the state's heritage. Recent volumes on southern gardens, plantation gardens, Mississippi Valley gardens, and "golden age" American gardens have included examples from Louisiana, because of their national and international historical significance and because of their striking scale and beauty. Yet whenever Louisiana gardens are gathered with their counterparts from other places, the comparisons seem forced. Because the state's gardens are simply unlike other American gardens, the juxtaposition does not elicit their subtle beauties and meanings.

These gardens have often been romanticized and magnified into emblems of an opulence and extravagance no longer possible. The idea underlying that, replete with references to gardenias and camellias, hoopskirts, and drinks on verandas, does not ring true for anyone who has lived and gardened in Louisiana. Certainly many of the state's gardens were feasible only because of great wealth and prosperity. But the historical record, the words of the garden makers themselves, and the pictorial representations from the period tell the entirely different story of gardens as places where people lived and worked. Gardening was an integral part of living in this landscape, and regardless of a person's economic or social station, gardens were central to life. The passage of the seasons and years was marked by the cycles of keeping a garden, and whether the work occupied a dozen slaves supervised by a plantation mistress or amounted only to one tenant farmer's wife raising truck crops, along with vegetables and flowers for her family, the tenor of garden making was always that of personal commitment, of planning for a bigger and better season, and of experimentation, whether ambitious or modest. Once the gardens are recognized as outdoor spaces occupied by people working to turn a shared vision of beauty and productivity into reality, they can no longer be deemed simple stage sets where the gentry strolled in their leisure, reviewing the rewards of a prosperous life. The gardens were the people's homes, as important for solace and security as their houses were for shelter. The gardens were links between the past and the future, holding the hope of rebirth and renewal in the face of the ups and downs of Louisiana's political and economic history.

This book brings the reader to the gardens of Louisiana both through the eye of an artist and photographer and through reflective attention by a student of Louisiana garden history. A. J. Meek sees the gardens as aesthetic compositions, as collages of texture, form, and color, and as interactions between nature and art. I look at the gardens as bearers of meaning, as manifestations of human stories about place and nature and human imagination. My particular interest is in the gardens as personal expressions of their makers and keepers—the people who envisioned the spaces, who labored to give them form, and who maintained them in the face of the climatic challenges that gardening in Louisiana presents: exuberant, almost overnight growth, extremes of temperature, seasonal tornadoes and hurricane-force storms, and more humidity and rainfall than would seem natural to many.

The state embodies the confluence of many cultures, climatic conditions, and physiographies, with the result that there is no typical Louisiana garden. From the earliest colonial gardens to the gardens of the antebellum past and on to those of recent years, what is striking is their amazing variety. The state's garden treasury not only reflects the differences in the cultural backgrounds of those involved in gardening over the centuries but also bespeaks the personalities of the inhabitants of the state—how they have thought about and acted upon their individual visions of what a garden can mean. For some, the prevailing style in a former homeland was the strongest design inspiration; for others, the peculiar qualities of a site shaped the garden. For many, the gardens brought together the ideas and labor of several generations of a family living in their personal landscape, gradually molding it to their needs and aspirations.

As distinctive as each garden is, Louisiana gardens share in a sense of tradition and heritage, of atmospheric density, and of fleeting beauty. It is the ephemeral quality of gardens that has moved so many novelists, poets, artists, musicians, and filmmakers to use them as the setting and point of departure for their creative works. At the same time, there is in gardens an affirmation of the continuity of culture, born of the awareness that gardens live on forever in one form or another. The gardens shown in this volume range from early examples that are now barely distinguishable from their surroundings, because of the change they have undergone, to the most recently built and meticulously maintained environments. But everywhere the power of place is evident.

Beyond evincing place and time, each garden bears a singular story of living in the landscape and acting out in it the deepest of conceits, ideals, and dreams. The garden of Aime lies in ruin not only because of the passage of over a century and a half but also because of the circumstances of Aime's life, which determined how he lived in his garden. In 1854, his only son, Gabriel, died suddenly of yellow fever at the age of twenty-eight. Aime wrote in his diary on the day of his son's death, "Let him who wishes continue. My time is finished." Since he withdrew from his beloved garden, it has been managed only by the cycle of nature: the spread of high waters after rains in spring, the verdant growth of vines in summer, the decay of fallen leaves in autumn, and the hibernation of mosquitoes and snakes in winter.

What makes it possible to relate these gardens to personal lives is an abundance of archival material, such as correspondence, diaries, journals, and business accounts, as well as contemporaneous pictorial resources, such as paintings, measured surveys, and photographs. All this provides a context for viewing the gardens Meek's camera lens reveals.

Photographer's Comment: A Homage to Eugène Atget

In Montparnasse, a dirty, rundown outlying section of Paris, a photographer rises before dawn. His wife lies sleeping. For breakfast he has a bowl of crumbled stale bread sprinkled with sugar, over which he has poured milk. He has this with his coffee. It is cold and wintry in the fall of 1901. Now fifty, he has been making photographs for only ten years, dedicating himself to photographing old Paris before it is lost—before the changes sure to come in the new century. For the next twenty years he will continue photographing his beloved city and its environs.

He is interested in preserving a wide range of subjects with his camera, from architectural details of buildings erected several centuries before to common street scenes. His great love is the parks and gardens, some already in decay and neglect. Above his door is a hand-painted sign advertising the wares from which he makes his living: Documents for Artists.

Carrying a heavy eight-by-ten wooden camera and tripod down from the fifth floor, he places the equipment in a large pushcart and walks all over the city to reach the places he wishes to photograph. On his rounds he meets vendors beginning their day or prostitutes ending theirs. He may stop to photograph a storefront. Stylish bowler hats float like surreal clouds in space while a mannequin appears to

Eugène Atget, *Trianon,* 1901

be looking for its lost head. He finds little-known parks, like St. Cloud and Sceaux, an entanglement of vines and overgrown brush. A statue points enigmatically to something hidden among the trees. It begins to rain, only slightly at first, then harder. He continues on. He makes a few more photographs.

On rare days he takes the Métro, as when he photographed the park at Versailles in the spring. That day was cloudy but bright. There was not another soul present, and his photographs here were usually devoid of people. Beginning at the palace, he photographed the reflecting pools and giant vases. Early morning fog burned off as he focused his camera on the many statues in the park. Shooting directly into the sun, he set up under a tree to avoid the lens flare that would ruin the picture. By the time afternoon shadows fell, he had exposed his plates for the day. He would catch the train back to Paris. The next morning he would develop and print the day's shooting.

Eugène Atget never had a book published or his work exhibited during his lifetime. His photographs might have been lost to us but for Bernice Abbott, an American photographer who was at the time working as an artist's assistant. She discovered and photographed Atget in 1927, a few months before his death.

Times have changed, yet some things remain the same. Atget's influence on my work cannot be denied. Photography stands on the threshold of a digital-imaging technical revolution. Still I make photographs the old-fashioned way, with a large-format wooden field camera, smaller than Atget's instrument but larger than most of my contemporaries'. Like Atget, I prefer overcast light, to reveal form and to provide a neutral gray sky as background. The gardens of Louisiana are farther south than any part of France, but visually there are similarities with the central France of Atget. There is the echo of an earlier aristocracy in both places. Louisiana's gardens in many ways spring from ideas similar to those behind the imperial designs of seventeenth- and eighteenth-century France, though on a smaller scale. These places leave me with a sense of discovery. I am interested in photographing the details that give a feel for the whole rather than adopting the more typical angle of view. I have enjoyed wandering through these places of contemplation and personal reflection. I think of others, from the past, who may have done the same in Gethsemane or Giverny. The sense of a presence remains with me and in the photographs.

The Gardens of LOUISIANA

American Rose Center

ELsong Garden

MAP OF

THE GARDENS OF LOUISIANA

PLACES of WORK and WONDER

Hodges Gardens

Afton Villa
Butler Greenwood • Rosedown
Oakley

Zemurray Gardens

Parlange • • Maison Chenal

Windrush Gardens

L'Hermitage
Houmas House

Shadows-on-the-Teche

Rip Van Winkle Gardens •
Jungle Gardens •

Le Petit Versailles

Longue Vue

New Orleans Botanical Garden
Beauregard-Keyes House
Hermann-Grima House

dave '97

Gardening in Louisiana: A Journey Through Time

To have a garden, which here is half of life.

—Adrien de Pauger, 1722

From Paris we dined at Versailles where we were shown the magnificent Palace of the King. There is enough there to satisfy anyone's curiosity and I often had the desire to close my eyes to mortify myself—this kind of mortification still costs me a great deal.

— *The Letters of Marie-Madeleine Hachard, Ursuline of New Orleans, 1727–1728*

EUROPEANS' ENCOUNTER WITH THE LANDSCAPE

Remembering that the reign of Louis XIV coincided with the early exploration and settlement of the territory of Louisiana, named for the monarch, assists in understanding the history of early gardens in the area. The designs of André Le Nôtre, the king's legendary garden architect and creator of both Vaux-le-Vicomte and Versailles, evidently left an imprint on the mind's eye of many a Frenchman who came to the New World to establish New France and reap the riches of the newfound territory. It was Louis who had authorized the establishment of a military outpost near the mouth of the Mississippi in 1697. The wealth that was eventually to support the planting of elegant gardens in Louisiana, however, was not the sort that the Spanish had been mining in New Spain. Apart from the colony's strategic military location, its principal basis for wealth was to be its abundant fertile soil. From the earliest explorations, Europeans had remarked on the lushness of the vegetation they observed. Pierre Lemoyne, sieur d'Iberville, a distinguished Canadian war hero who headed France's expedition to the lower Mississippi to carry out Louis' intention, recorded in his journal for 1699 the impression the natural beauty and fecundity of the indigenous

forest were making on him: "The beautiful countryside is blanketed by woods, containing all varieties of trees, except pines. I have seen a few wild apple trees and a few peach trees; there are neither strawberries, raspberries, nor mulberries." Later in the journey, he described the effort required in getting the timber to build a settlement. He said that it took an entire day to cut a single tree, selected mostly from oaks and pecans. He complained that he had to set up a forge to repair the axes that "break without exception." But once construction was moving forward, he could assign "twenty-five men to sowing peas, maize, and beans." The choice of crops took its cue from the local Indians.

There are no lands cultivated the whole length of the river, only great wild forests inhabited solely by beasts of all colors, serpents, adders, scorpions, crocodiles, vipers, toads, and others which did us no harm even though they came quite near us.

—The Letters of Marie-Madeleine Hachard, Ursuline of New Orleans, 1727–1728

Iberville's description of what his men had to do—clear the forest, build from the timber, and plant staple food crops—prefigures the experience of later settlers approaching the wilderness of Louisiana and attempting to carve a place for civilization out of the pervasive forest. Although the forest held a store of timber and of plant species, it was first and foremost an impediment to settlement. The first months and perhaps years of most settlers' tenancy had to be spent clearing land. Once that was done and dwellings were constructed, the next task was to plant. The paramount thought had to be of survival, and orchards and kitchen gardens were the means to that.

The pattern during the eighteenth century and into the nineteenth of clearing land that the settlers thought of as wild affected their preferences regarding gardens. Although by the early eighteenth century the English romantic landscape was à la mode in France, a soft, naturalistic landscape held little appeal on the newly settled frontier, where order and security meant removing as much of nature as possible.

URBAN BEGINNINGS AND SUBURBAN VILLAS

New Orleans . . . is situated on the left bank a hundred miles from the mouth of the river. Far from standing on an elevated position, the city is built, on the contrary, on swampy foundations, lower than the level of the river, and which would be constantly submerged were it not for the levees, that are built and kept at great expense.

—Marie Fontenay de Grandfort, *The New World* (1855)

There are few towns on the surface of the globe possessing such a medley of population as New Orleans. There are five distinct bases to the mixed race that inhabits it—the Anglo-American, the French, the Spanish, the African, and the Indian. Not only is each of these to be found in it unmixed with any other, but they are all commingled, the one with the other, in a variety of ways and in interminable degrees.

—Alexander Mackay, *The Western World* (1849)

The first permanent European settlement in the lower Mississippi Valley was at Natchitoches, on the Red River, in 1714, but the only outpost of the early settlement period to assume features of a major urban center was New Orleans. In 1717, Jean Baptiste Lemoyne, sieur de Bienville, a French Canadian, selected a site for the city, which was to be a trading post and administrative center for the French. The location had a commanding view up and down the Mississippi, and breezes from the river could moderate the subtropical heat. Most important, Bayou St. John and an Indian portage enabled passage between Lake Pontchartrain and the river.

The city was to become and remain unlike any other on the new continent. A virtual Paris in the wilderness, it enjoyed all the landscape and planning advantages that distinguish great cities: broad tree-lined avenues, and public squares on which churches and public buildings faced, as well as a layout that pointed the way toward harmonious expansion while responding to the natural lay of the land and the river. And it had the rich alluvial soil and abundant rainfall conducive to making gardening an inseparable part of its culture.

But the site was also less than ideal in many ways. Much of the city was below sea level, so that high water and flooding were constant concerns. Hurricanes and tropical storms bore down on the city, and the extreme summer heat and humidity made it susceptible to epidemics. Nevertheless, New Orleans was to be one of the most successful urban experiments in North America. It in effect controlled the trade of the Mississippi Valley. And its public landscape and luxuriant private gardens have always set it apart.

The Vieux Carre, or French Quarter, was the original colonial town and is now the heart of the city. The Place d'Armes, today's Jackson Square, was at the center facing the river, and the streets and residential blocks followed a gridiron plan that was to determine the positioning of gardens in residential properties. Adrien de Pauger, who had been sent to supervise the surveying and laying-out of the grid, described in 1722 his recommendation for the parceling of individual lots: "I have . . . indicated the distribution of some of the lots on this plan . . . in order to proportion them to the faculties of the inhabitants and of such size that each and every one may have the houses on the street front and may still have some land in the rear to have a garden, which here is half of life." The climate was both a blessing and a curse for gardeners as they began experimenting with the ways of the soil in the new landscape. The indigenous flora may have seemed paradisiacal to many, but its thickness and vigor must have been daunting too. The French learned from the Indians how to plant so as to have at hand the foodstuffs they needed. With the arrival of settlers from other European countries and the growth of the slave population, kitchen gardening in the city adopted even more diverse practices.

The narrow and deep lots were fenced and walled from the earliest days. A decree of 1722 warned that "all inhabitants of this place

Our residence since our arrival here is the finest house in the city. It has two stories and a garret. We have all the apartments we need with six doors to enter those on the ground floor. . . . Our residence is located at one end of the city. We have a poultry yard and a garden bounded on one side and end by large wilderness trees of prodigious height and breadth. . . .

We also eat watermelons and French melons and sweet potatoes which are large roots that are cooked in the coals like chestnuts. They even taste sweet like chestnuts but are much sweeter, very soft and very good. . . .

Regarding the fruits of the country, there are many that we do not care for but the peaches and figs are very excellent and abundant. We are sent so many of them from the nearby plantations that we make them into preserves and jelly. Blackberry jelly is particularly good. Reverend Father de Beaubois has the finest garden in the city. It is full of oranges which bear as beautiful and as sweet an orange as those of Cape Francis. He gave us three hundred sour ones which we preserved. . . . Our principal aim is to attract souls to the Lord and He accords us graces so that we can perform this duty.

—*The Letters of Marie-Madeleine Hachard*

must have their houses or land enclosed by palisades within two months or else they will be deprived of their property." The enclosures imparted a sense of visual order and prevented animals from wandering onto properties. They also sustained a sense of privacy as houses came to be built on smaller and smaller lots and were crowded together with party walls.

The earliest gardens of the French Quarter were simple corollaries of the urban grid, usually rectangular. Period maps of the Quarter show buildings symmetrically arranged around the Place d'Armes, with large gardens, each comprising four squares, behind them. The Gonichon plan of 1731 includes the expansion of the Quarter and depicts most of the gardens as rectangles divided into four quadrants, with the quadrants subdivided by diagonals. Simple geometric shapes had characterized urban gardens in Europe since the Middle Ages. Combining such shapes permitted footpaths for maintenance and strolling, and yielded planting beds suited to the universal system of row cultivation.

Among the first gardens described in existing documents from the time is one at the Ursuline Convent, at the northern extreme of the French Quarter and today a property of the archdiocese of New Orleans. Since the garden does not survive, the written description furnishes our only knowledge of it. In 1727, a group of Ursuline nuns had come to New Orleans from France to work as missionaries and operate a boarding school for young girls. By 1734, their

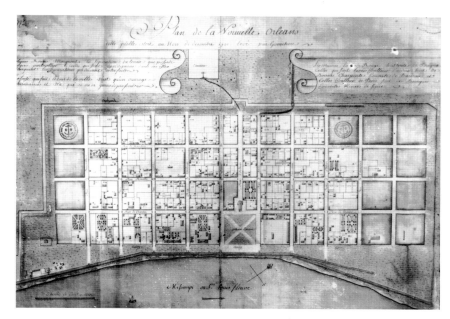

Plan of New Orleans such as it was in the month of December, 1731, drawn by Gonichon. The plan shows the substantial space devoted to gardens in the early days of the French colonial city.

permanent convent was completed, and shortly afterward they planted a medicinal garden, which presumably complemented an orchard and a kitchen garden, or *potager*. The published letters of one of the nuns offer insight into the importance plants had for setting an adequate table. Other documents from the first half of the eighteenth century make clear that the successful cultivation of vegetables and fruit trees was the overriding concern and preoccupation of every gardener—and presumably, all families gardened.

Unlike colonial gardens along the eastern seaboard, in which the cultivation of herbs was a great preoccupation, the gardens in

The vegetable market is one of the best I ever saw. The meat market except in the article of mutton is very poor. . . . Both markets were well filled with sellers and buyers, and there were plenty of females with long black veils, some pretty enough—and others ugly and old. Numbers of old colored women in Angola shawls were seated on the pavement with vegetables for sale before them. They were picturesque enough in their bright headdresses and with their polite manners and rapid enunciation. French, in the market, as on the levee, was the language predominant in sound.

—John H. B. Latrobe, *Southern Travels* (1834)

I wish you would ask Fanny Conrad to get some dried sage. It is impossible to get any here or in the Attakapas.

—Mary Clara Weeks Moore to John Moore, who was in Baton Rouge, March 8, 1850

south Louisiana appear seldom to have given much space to herbs. At least the records rarely mention them. The garden at the Ursuline Convent may be the only garden of the state's colonial period for which there is evidence of a specialization in herbs. Because the nuns' mission was not only to educate young girls but to serve the sick, a plot of herbs for medicinal use was appropriate, continuing a tradition that extended back to medieval cloisters. But to grow herbs for the typical domestic kitchen in the French Quarter would have been far less sensible. The French Market abounded with common and exotic herbs and spices from abroad, and herbs and tender cool-weather perennials cannot do well where a high water table, like that of New Orleans, keeps roots wet most of the time, even in raised beds. When the torrential rainstorms of summer afternoons hit the saturated soil and then the hot sun breaks through, herb plants are likely to be quite literally cooked, if they are not first drowned. If herbs were not typically a major part of kitchen gardens, it also seems from the documentation that kitchen gardens may themselves have ceased to be standard for the Quarter's courtyards, at least after the end of the eighteenth century. As the neighborhood became more densely populated, already-narrow lots were subdivided, rendering kitchen gardens impracticable. Most residents were of the mercantile class, anyway. They were more apt to invest time in business and the routines of the city's social life than in productive tilling of the soil. More likely, their gardens combined ornamentals and fragrant blooming plants, including the trees that produced fresh fruit for the table at the same time that they perfumed the air.

All of the houses here, except some in the old town and centre streets, have gardens—not very extensive . . . but the soil and climate are such that everything grows luxuriantly. Magnolias, jessamines, roses, oranges, lemons, loquats, and a hundred other things beautiful and good; and then the mocking birds and butterflies, and the pretty little chameleons!

—Amelia M. Murray, *Letters from the United States, Cuba, and Canada* (1856)

The nineteenth-century gardens of New Orleans have been more thoroughly and accurately recorded than those of any other American city, through the measured plans and elevations in the New Orleans Notarial Archives. Over five thousand properties were drawn to scale by engineers, surveyors, and artists in connection with judicially ordered property sales. The magnificent watercolor posters in the archives, now housed

Plan of a residence in the French Quarter, 1853, showing large garden on lot to left of house. The structure at the far bottom left of this garden is probably a greenhouse.

Plan Book 62, folio 8, C. A. de Armas, 1853, New Orleans Notarial Archives; Customhouse Street between Burgundy and Rampart Streets, backed by Canal Street.

in the New Orleans City Hall, give a sense of the courtyards and gardens hidden from passersby behind walls and fences.

Garden plans ranged from long, narrow utilitarian rectangles surrounded by paved walkways to elaborate geometric parterres. Occasionally a large number of beds and a structure that looks like a greenhouse appear in a plan, but that is rare and may have been for the few florists in business in the early-nineteenth-century city.

In 1838, J. F. Lelièvre, a Frenchman living in New Orleans and formerly the gardener-agriculturist of the colonial French government, published a book of instructions for "persons occupied in gardening." *Nouveau Jardinier de la Louisiane* is a handbook and an almanac, with an extensive list of flowers and vegetables and considerations about their culture. Lelièvre argued that the New Orleans gardener should not shun flowers: "If the plants about which I have just written are interesting for their utility, then the flowers merit equal attention from the amateur. They are the most beautiful ornament of a garden, and add infinite value to country life, both by the variety of colors and by the sweetness of the perfume that they exude. The culture of flowers is one of the principal branches of the art of gardening, and the most difficult." The book promoted a broad variety of flowers, vegetables, and fruits, which presumably were available to residents. In particular, the growing of fruit was widespread, not only because it contributed to a good diet but also because it was easy in the subtropical climate. In 1796, Joseph de Pontalba, a resident of New Orleans, wrote to his wife in France about their garden in the city, which he had been forced to sell: "I walked all about it and everywhere I found something that brought back your presence. . . . I found all my fruit trees in good shape, all the grafts I had made are bearing, vines covered with grapes; it has more fruit than leaves. I am persuaded that one could count more than six thousand bunches of grapes on it."

The courtyard of the Hermann-Grima House was not recorded in the archives, but its tall brick walls concealing everything from the street and its layout of long, narrow rectangular beds are typical of many of the gardens illustrated there. The garden of the Beauregard-Keyes House, which was recorded in 1865, had an unusual design for the antebellum period. Between the main house and the outbuildings, or dependencies, where there were often planted beds, the drawings show a simple grid of trees, apparently an orchard. Perhaps it consisted of dwarf trees, which were superior for a tight space and where having the fruit within reach mattered. Occupying the entire lot to the left of the house was a large formal garden—a rectangle divided into four quadrants with a central circle of plants. Behind that parterre was a long and narrow structure, probably an arbor. Although this garden was destroyed in the nineteenth century, it was reconstructed in the mid–twentieth century on the basis of the measured survey.

The courtyard garden of the Gallier House was designed by James Gallier, Jr., an architect for several memorable buildings in the city, including the Opera House, erected in 1859. Gallier had toured Europe with his father, also an architect, in the 1840s and had seen

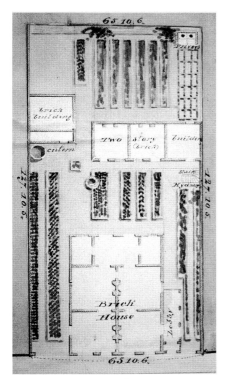

Plan of a residence in the French Quarter near the Hermann-Grima House, 1856. Planted beds in the first court are not of uniform width, as in the Hermann-Grima courtyard. The dependencies separate the first court from the back court, which is also furnished with long, rectangular beds. Privies are at top right corner; the structure in front of them is probably an arbor, perhaps for grapes.

Plan Book 44, folio 41, C. A. de Armas, 1856, New Orleans Notarial Archives; St. Louis Street between Burgundy and Dauphine Streets, backed by Conti Street.

Drawing of the garden of a Creole cottage in New Orleans, 1858. The garden is laid out with long, rectangular beds that are planted with uniform rows of either shrubs or small trees. In the reconstruction of the Hermann-Grima courtyard in the 1980s, this drawing constituted part of the basis for planting kumquat trees in uniform rows in some of the beds.

Plan Book 48, folio 64, signed Tourné and de L'Isle, 1858, New Orleans Notarial Archives; Morales Street between Frenchmen Street and Elysian Fields Avenue, backed by Urquhart Street.

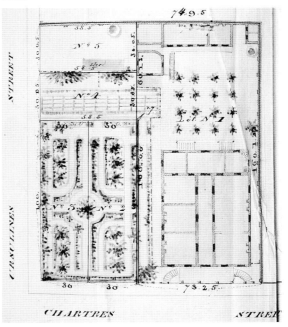

Plan of the Beauregard-Keyes House displaying its courtyard and garden, 1865.

E. Bouny, Volume VII, Act 13, 1865, New Orleans Notarial Archives; 1101–1113 Chartres Street.

some of the great buildings of the world. For the courtyard of his own residence he sketched out a narrow rectangular grass panel, labeled "Grass plot of Bermuda grass," that was intersected with a round basin he marked as a "water closet sink hole." It is not clear whether this had been transformed into a fountain by the time the courtyard was built or whether the fountain is more recent. The earliest known photograph of the court, from 1907, fifty years after the construction of the house, shows the basin filled in and planted with ornamentals. Flagstone paths surround the grass. In Gallier's sketch—the only drawing of a pre–Civil War French Quarter garden by its designer so far discovered—a raised area along the side of the narrow rectangular court is marked "flower box" or "flower bed." The decision to devote most of the tight usable space of the courtyard to an ornamental feature like a lawn panel was unprecedented in the Quarter, since as a rule it was needed as an outdoor work area. Perhaps the architect's appreciation of European formality played a part in his decision to design the space in this way.

It is the survival of so many of these remarkable courtyards that has made the French Quarter the legendary tourist attraction it is today. Throughout this century, the courtyards have inspired painters, photographers, novelists, and filmmakers to celebrate in art the character of the neighborhood. The mixture with the predominant French stock of Spanish, German, and other European as well as African and West Indian lineages, produced an exceptional richness of garden ideas. And the neighborhood as a whole has managed to retain the feeling of its French roots to a degree unparalleled anywhere else outside France itself.

The French carried to the New World not only their ideas about the layout of residential gardens but also their grand tradition of urban design and municipal open space. Unlike many frontier settlements, New Orleans was mapped out to include numerous public squares in the residential quarters, and wide boulevards generously planted with trees. In the years immediately after the Louisiana Purchase, in 1803, the French retained their hold on the older parts of the city, but Americans from the eastern seaboard and from other southern states began to move to New Orleans in great numbers. They settled farther upriver in sections now known as the Lower Garden District and the Garden District. In these areas, suburban at the time, large villas and mansions went up, with ornamental plantings in the front and often on one side, the properties surrounded by fences of wood or iron. Lots were significantly larger than in the Quarter, and plans in the Notarial Archives from the new neighborhoods trace a departure from the tight formal geometry of downtown courtyards to a looser, more naturalistic approach re-

Plan of the Gallier House, drawn by James Gallier, Jr., in 1852, showing layout of courtyard with grass plot and basin.

Original in private collection; reproduction in Gallier House.

It suffices to say that there is a song sung openly here in which the words proclaim that this city is as beautiful as Paris. Does that not explain to you how the people feel?

—*The Letters of Marie-Madeleine Hachard*

The public square which is open to the river has an admirable general effect, and is infinitely superior to any thing in our atlantic cities as a water view of the city. . . . The square itself is neglected, the fences ragged, and in many places open. Part of it is let for a depot for firewood, paving stones are heaped up in it, and along the whole of the side next the river is a row of mean booths in which dry goods are sold. . . . Thus a square, which might be made the handsomest in America, is really rather a nuisance than other wise.

—Benjamin Henry Latrobe, on the Place d'Armes, 1819

We turned down Canal Street—the broadest in New Orleans, and destined to be the most magnificent. . . . Through its center runs a double row of young trees, which, when they arrive at maturity, will form the finest mall in the United States.

—Joseph Holt Ingraham, *Travels in the Southwest by a Yankee* (1835)

Drawing of a house in the Garden District, 1870, illustrating the new expansiveness and openness of gardens in the American sector. Notice the ornamental fountain in the side yard.

Plan Book 97, folio 19, J. A. Celles, 1870, New Orleans Notarial Archives; Jackson Street, corner of Prytania Street, backed by Philip Street and St. Charles Avenue.

sponsive to the ideas on garden design that Andrew Jackson Downing enunciated beginning in the 1840s. Because of the gardens' size and their variety of high-maintenance plants and because of their many changes of ownership during the ups and downs of inner-city neighborhoods, few if any from this so-called American sector have survived in their nineteenth-century form. Most of the gardens and landscapes in today's Garden District date from the 1920s, the 1950s, or the last ten years or so. There is renewed interest in the landscape of the Garden District, and it is renowned for its luxuriant, shady, and mostly evergreen gardens. At first these gardens were probably for the most part sunny, with small shade trees planted at the periphery, but now the trees envelop most of the properties in deep and cool shade, producing settings of an altogether distinctive character. Instead of full-sun gardens of colorful flowering annuals and perennials, there are shrubs and ground covers forming a dark green carpet beneath huge live oaks.

New Orleans was and is the landscape with the most extensive and most remarkable urban configuration in the state. But there were other urban areas in Louisiana where the kinds of layouts and garden designs adopted in New Orleans also gained acceptance and where sophisticated concepts of open space were embraced. Baton Rouge, which would become the state capital and an impor-

tant commercial center by virtue of being the deepwater port farthest upriver on the Mississippi, began with a grid plan and a dock and market area along the waterfront, like New Orleans. The city developed by spreading out from there. In 1806, alert to the prospect of urban growth, an entrepreneur, Elias Beauregard, proposed an enclave adjacent to the city center and had a French engineer draw up a plan patterned on the axial formality of French models. The plan placed the cathedral in a square at the center, the Place Royal, from which four diagonal streets radiated. Six other public squares added to the open space of the scheme. In the newspaper announcement of the development, Beauregard described his plans for the central street: "The middle part of the town is to be crossed by a large street 100 feet wide, with trees planted on each side, at the end of which stands a Government House, which looks out on the Place d'Armes, the Barracks, and the Queen's Walk, Court la Reine, a prolonging of the above wide street." Public buildings were to be positioned throughout the neighborhood in order to "afford a more uniform value to all the lots, and to contribute at the same time to general convenience and ornament." The streets were built according to Beauregard's plan, but when the lots did not sell as hoped, the scheme was abandoned. Today the Place d'Eglise is cut in half by a state highway. But the scale of Beauregard's plan, with its four diagonal

Baton Rouge is a village charmingly situated on the eastern bank of the Mississippi, one hundred and fifty miles above New Orleans. . . . On the parade stands a beautiful monument of white marble consecrated to the memory of some officers of the garrison, who deceased there. It is not an expensive, but very striking monument. . . . The town itself, rising with such a fine swell from the river, with its singularly shaped French and Spanish houses, and green squares, looked in the distance like a fine landscape painting.

—Timothy Flint, *Recollections of the Last Ten Years in the Valley of the Mississippi* (1826)

From the esplanade there is an extensive and commanding prospect of the inland country—the extended shores, stretching out north and south, dotted with elegant villas, and richly enamelled by their high state of cultivation. . . . The view of the town from the deck of the steamer is highly beautiful. The rich, green swells rising gradually from the water—its pleasant streets, bordered with the umbrageous China tree—its colonnaded dwellings—its mingled town and rural scenery, and its pleasant suburbs, give it an air of quiet and novel beauty, such as one loves to gaze upon in old landscapes which the imagination fills with ideal images of its own.

—Joseph Holt Ingraham, *Travels in the Southwest by a Yankee*

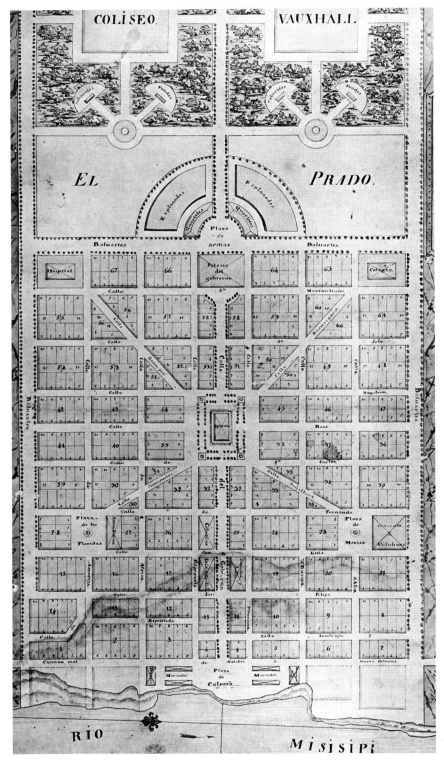

Plan of Baton Rouge's second suburb and first planned community, Beauregard Town, 1806.

Facsimile (Baton Rouge, n.d.) of *Plano de la villa de Baton Rouge trazada sobre la habitación del Sr. E. Beauregard por A. Lacarrière Latour en novembre 1806.*

streets, has created a character distinct from that of other American neighborhoods.

Other, smaller quasi-urban localities in the state served as centers of distribution for plantation crops and provided mercantile amenities. What made each of these towns and villages viable were the great plantations encircling them. Despite the distances separating rural and urban settlements, there was constant communication between the planters and their agents and brokers, and between the gentry living in the country and the merchants with fine goods in the towns. The waterways were the threads that connected town and country and that people and goods followed back and forth. The rivers and bayous were filled with the traffic of life in early Louisiana and were the real arteries for the flow of both commerce and society.

PLANTATION GARDENS

For some miles after leaving New Orleans, the eye rests agreeably on scenes of fine sugar and cotton plantations which border the stream. They are embellished with orange groves, in the center of which are located the snow white mansions of the planters. There are avenues of oaks, cedars, and magnolias, numerous bearing pecan trees, and hedges of osage orange and cherokee rose. Little by little, the houses and gardens lessen in number, but all the way to Baton Rouge, one continues to see fine lands well cultivated.

—A. Levasseur, *Lafayette in America* (1829)

The lives of many in antebellum Louisiana spanned city and country. While New Orleans was becoming a booming center for trade, the surrounding lands that had been awarded as concessions to European settlers were evolving into great plantations. In a painting of New Orleans from the year of the Louisiana Purchase, there are not only the densely inhabited French Quarter, the Mississippi full of merchant ships, and the commerce and society of the levee but also, in the corner, the garden of Marigny plantation. The artist was conscious of the interdependence of city and country.

In carving cultivable acreage from the forested banks of the river, the work and risk were considerable. Indigo, the first cash crop, was soon superseded by sugarcane, in the wetter lands, and cotton, adjacent to the higher reaches of the river. Along with hundreds

A View of New Orleans from the plantation of Marigny, by J. L. Boqueta de Woiseri, 1803. The painting shows the intimate connection of the young city and its rural plantations at the time of the Louisiana Purchase.

of acres of cash croplands, the plantation landscape included levees along the rivers and bayous, networks of drainage ditches, quarters housing slave laborers, and barns, stables, and sheds for field animals and equipment. In the case of sugarcane plantations, mills were necessary as well.

One of the first needs in establishing a plantation was siting the main house and laying out the gardening plots. The principal dwelling was usually placed at the highest point, for the prevailing breezes and security from flooding, with a prospect over river, bayou, or road, as well as fields and mill, or sugarhouse. Although most renderings of plantation complexes represent the "big house" as the keystone, on a sugar plantation the main house usually shared visual prominence with the sugarhouse, on which the family depended for its fortune.

The gardens most important to the planter and his family were the kitchen garden and the orchard, for the daily food they supplied. These were under the supervision of the mistress of the plantation and were tended by

By a peculiarity perhaps unique, the highest places in all these lands are the banks of the Mississippi and of the bayous, as well as the shores of the lakes. This high ground provides the only means they have of establishing plantations; and it generally consists of good soil, rarely with too much clay in it.

—James Pitot, *Observations on the Colony of Louisiana from 1796 to 1802* (1802)

slaves, male and female. Little site evidence has survived, however, and most of the archival documents touching on gardens mention the plants grown in them, not their form and location. One valuable source of information about the siting of kitchen gardens in the Deep South, however, is the *Southern Rural Almanac, and Plantation and Garden Calendar,* by Thomas Affleck, published in annual editions from about 1851 to 1860. Affleck's instructions on planting in New Orleans and Natchez recognized the significant differences between subtropical south Louisiana and the temperate zone lying northward from about Baton Rouge. The 1860 edition carried highly specific advice about layout. The author recommended a spot with a gentle downward slope to the east and protection from "cold, north blasts," along with proximity to a water source and a source of manure. He continued,

> The location should be one convenient to the dwelling, that the ladies of the family may have easy access; the garden being usually under their exclusive care. . . .
>
> The shape should be an oblong square, that the plow and cultivator may be used as much as possible. One broad main walk up the centre, at least eight feet wide, with a gate at each end, wide enough for a cart or wagon to pass; with borders five feet wide next the fence, all around; and a walk inside of these borders, also five feet wide. Dwarfed fruit trees may be planted alongside of the walks. . . . The less complication in the arrangement and laying off the vegetable garden, the better. Shade and ornamental trees, flower, etc. are out of place here.

Affleck commented that the kitchen garden was almost never cared for by plantation hands. Rather, house servants looked after it during their "leisure time."

Between the house and the street was a yard, planted formally with orange trees and other evergreens. A little on one side of the house stood a large two-story, square dovecote, which is a universal appendage of a sugar planter's house. In the rear of the house was another large yard, in which, irregularly placed, were houses for the family servants, a kitchen, stable, carriage house, smokehouse, etc. Behind this rear yard there was a vegetable garden, of an acre or more, in the charge of a Negro gardener; a line of fig trees were planted along the fence, but all the ground enclosed was intended to be cropped with vegetables for the family, and for the supply of "the people." I was pleased to notice, however, that the Negro gardener had, of his own accord, planted some violets and other flowering plants.

—Frederick Law Olmsted, *The Cotton Kingdom* (1861)

Curiously, the terms *kitchen garden* and *vegetable garden* seem to have been little used at the time in writing of plantations, if they were used at all. The term in currency was simply *garden,* leaving

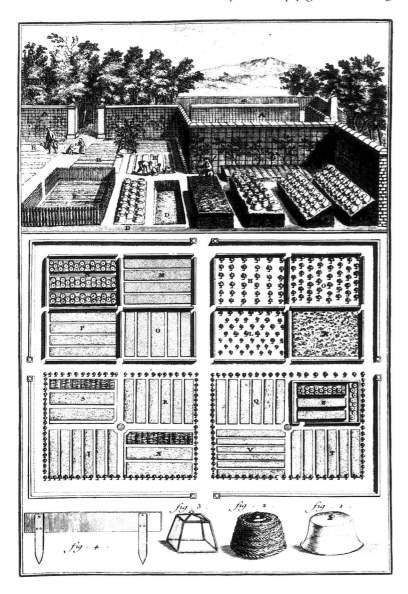

Jardin Potager Couches, a plate in Diderot's *Encyclopédie, 1762–1777,* published as a document of science and technology at the start of the Industrial Revolution. Louisiana kitchen gardens were surrounded not by masonry walls but rather by wooden fences, but the use of row cultivation and the arrangement of rectangular plots in a layout of four squares were common in Louisiana. Glass *cloches,* or bell jars, were employed in Louisiana gardens to shield tender seedlings, in just the way illustrated here.

Denis Diderot, *Recueil de planches, sur les sciences, les arts libéraux, et les arts mécaniques, avec leur explication* (New York, 1969), 30.

the modern reader to figure out exactly what kind of garden was involved.

Nor are there many graphic depictions from which information about antebellum kitchen gardens can be gleaned. A plate in Denis Diderot's *Encyclopédie* entitled "Garden with Walls Supporting Espaliers" gives an idea of the French precedent for such gardens, though it must be remembered that masonry walls did not enclose those on Louisiana plantations. But the overall clarity of the rectilinear layout in the plate and the central and perimeter paths are in line with the scant evidence we have about Louisiana. The painting *A Louisiana Plantation,* in which Adrien Persac in 1861 depicted the plantation of Chevalier Delhomme, in St. Martin Parish, shows what is almost certainly a similar rectilinear kitchen garden in the foreground across from the front of the house. Persac, a French draftsman and architect, settled in New Orleans in 1857 and painted a series of gouaches of Louisiana plantation houses between his arrival and 1861. In that year he was commissioned to paint double portraits of Shadows-on-the-Teche. In the foreground of the one of the front of the mansion are beds like those in the painting of Delhomme's plantation.

A more stylized and simplified kitchen garden appears behind a

A Louisiana Plantation, by Adrien Persac, 1861. In this St. Martin Parish plantation's kitchen garden (foreground), small trees, perhaps dwarf fruit trees, provide some shade for tender vegetable plantings below.

Louisiana State Museum

house in documents from 1850 in the New Orleans Notarial Archives recording a rural property near the city. A perspective drawing shows two fenced yards behind the dwelling, the first the kitchen or service yard, the other, with three outbuildings, the kitchen garden. This watercolor shows the square plots in different shades of brown and green to indicate plots of different vegetables.

I have my orchard planted with better than four hundred young fruit trees. I did not think I had so many friends. The people sent me trees from all quarters untill the ground was filled. It adds much to the beauty of the place.

—Rachel O'Connor (seventy years old), Bayou Sarah, to William Weeks, New Town, February 24, 1844

My new orchard is my idol. I am afraid I think too much of it, and that God will punish me for letting my heart cling to earthly treasures.

—Rachel O'Connor to William Weeks, March 23, 1844

Illustrations of orchards are even rarer than those of kitchen gardens. Whether a plantation had an orchard in traditional grid form or just small trees among the vegetable plots seems to have depended on the number of trees. *A Louisiana Plantation* has fruit trees interspersed; two drawings in the New Orleans Notarial Archives of plantations outside the city portray large grid orchards, each behind a house and its yard.

Plantation papers and diaries are the best sources for learning about the kinds of vegetables cultivated in Louisiana kitchen gardens. The diary of Martha Turnbull is particularly thorough in listing plants and the annual cycles of their culture. The mistress of Rosedown plantation, Turnbull kept an almost daily record of her kitchen and ornamental gardening from about 1834 until her death in 1896. But the correspondence of virtually any of the women in planters' families will mention something about the kitchen garden—the effect the weather has had on the plants or what is in bloom or what quantities of fruit and vegetables have been picked for the table. Allie Weeks Meade wrote to her mother at Shadows-on-the-Teche on August 14, 1854, "It is rather a bad time for gardening. . . . I want [rain] for the crops and garden, but I do not want it for getting wood. . . . The cabbage seed you sent me came up beautifully and are growing very finely. No one down this

Spring lettuce, Egg Plants & Radishes came up. Forked up my asparagus beds. Planted Parsnips, Carrots, Beets, & Salsify seed.

—Martha Turnbull Garden Diary, February 8, 1837

Paintings by Adrien Persac of Shadows-on-the-Teche, New Iberia, 1861. In the view of the house from the town, what may be a kitchen garden is in the foreground, as in the painting by Persac of the St. Martin Parish plantation. In the view from the bayou, dependencies dot the work yard, but it is possible to detect several ornamental plantings among the utilitarian structures.

Collection of Shadows-on-the-Teche, New Iberia

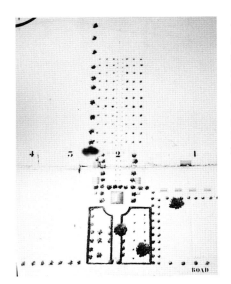

way has any garden. All are preparing fall garden. I have mustard, cabbage, pole beans, tomatoes and turnips coming on but are not yet bearing. . . . We are eating sweet potatoes, a very nice dish now is the young green pumpkins boiled with a piece of pork."

The *Nouveau Jardinier de la Louisiane* that Lelièvre produced in 1838 in New Orleans is the earliest known listing of cultivated plants, including vegetables, published in the state. The catalogs and order ledgers for Southern Nurseries, the retail business run by Affleck, suggest that fruit trees were among the most popular plants on the state's plantations. The catalog for 1851–1852 listed 215 varieties of pears, 177 of apples, 54 of peaches, and 21 of grapes. Travelers' accounts, particularly those regarding the New Orleans area, frequently mentioned hedges of orange trees around plantations.

Typically, plantation houses had an ornamental garden in front, for the most part a simple grid of trees or parterre, if paintings and drawings are indicative. Sometimes ornamental dovecotes, or *pigeonniers,* flanked the entrance to the house and served as small garden pavilions. *Pigeonniers* were much more common on plantations established by the French than on others. The frontispiece landscape was surrounded by a high white wooden fence both functional and ornamental. Often an elaborate gateway aligned with the central axis of the house led from the garden to either the road or the river. On river and bayou properties, there were usually landings or docks where steamboats delivered passengers, mail, and provisions and loaded cash crops for shipping to market. Some recently

discovered watercolors done in St. Charles Parish in the 1850s by Father Joseph Paret, a French Jesuit, reveal much about river landings, despite the priest's naïve style. The paintings also confirm that, at least in St. Charles Parish, grids of trees constituted the most common arrangement for ornamental gardens. But Paret recorded exceptions to the norm, as well: a circular driveway symmetrically flanked by plantings, and an open lawn balanced with two great trees. Typically, Paret painted the plantation complexes as seen from the river, but in the case of his own residence, the Presbytère, he painted both a front and a back view. Behind his house was an extensive fenced utility yard, and within that enclosure his kitchen garden. A passage in a letter he wrote to his brother in France reveals the priest's attempt to achieve something like the high-style French garden by using vegetable plantings to simulate borders of ornamental flowers:

> Feeling the need to stretch my legs and get a little fresh air, I left my easy chair and my pen to go amuse myself counting the different vegetables I've had planted now.
>
> I wish you could see this immense garden, how proper and charming it is. Without vanity, I believe that our inhabitants of St. Charles will be a little jealous. All the walks, all the squares are laid out with

Myrtle Land Plantation, by Father Joseph Paret, 1853. In this watercolor of a property in St. Charles Parish the sizable front garden consists of a central avenue lined by conically shaped evergreen trees, and side gardens of tree grids. Vine-covered arbors flank the big house, and the yard and its outbuildings are visible behind.

Presbytère, by Father Joseph Paret, 1853. Father Paret's watercolor portrait of the backyard of his own residence in St. Charles Parish shows the juxtaposition of his formally conceived kitchen garden and the chicken yard and dependencies.

Collection of Marcel Boyer, Givors, France

a string line. More than 3000 onions border the beds of this garden, looking like jonquils, tulips, Sweet Williams, and 700 endives, leaf lettuce and head lettuce, masquerading as hyacinths or ranunculi, border the ditches I had dug to catch the waters from heaven on stormy days.

Last December in the main walks and those that go all round this immense garden which forms a perfect square, I had them plant 488 trees: oranges, peaches and pomegranates, chinaberries, plums, persimmons, magnolias, mulberries, roses and altheas. This should give Father some desire to come visit me, but no, even the California gold mines would not tempt him.

Behind the house, a fenced yard was standard, with outbuildings at the perimeter. The fences were strictly utilitarian and either unpainted or a rough kind of white picket fence. The yard's appurtenances were those necessary for the daily operation of the big house: the kitchen, animal coops and pens, storehouses for provisions, the woodpile, the smokehouse, the blacksmith shop, quarters for house servants, privies, the laundry space, the animal rendering area, and the like. In keeping with functional objectives, the ground was often rid of vegetation and maintained as compacted or swept soil.

Beyond the yard were the plantation's larger structures, including a carriage house and livestock barns. Sometimes there were two barns, one near the main house for the carriage horses and milk cows, and the other nearer the sugarhouse for the mules and oxen deployed in cultivating, harvesting, hauling, and grinding sugarcane. There might also be a family cemetery and a schoolhouse.

Often greenhouses, cold frames, and hotbeds near the kitchen garden were used for the propagation of young vegetables and ornamentals and helped winter over tender container plants, like geraniums and begonias.

Affleck was not as sophisticated about ornamental gardens as he was about orchards and kitchen gardens. Although he dealt above all in fruit trees, he took some interest in promoting picturesque approaches to gardening. It is likely that he was familiar with Andrew Jackson Downing's writings—his periodical *The Horticulturist* or the seminal work he published in 1841, *A Treatise on the Theory and Practice of Landscape Gardening, Adapted*

Planted three dwarf banana trees in the middle of the hotbed frame, and six around the frame on September 1st; two were already in the middle, having been planted there by George in April. . . . A bunch of dwarf bananas contains 150 bananas and weighs 48 pounds.

—"Plantation Diary of the Late Mr. Valcour Aime," September, 1848

Put down corn. Greenhouse in order. Sewed Beets. . . . Still putting down box cuttings and trimed down the Wild Peach hedge to 14 inches. Set out Pinks sown in October and all kinds of flowers.

—Martha Turnbull Garden Diary, January 20–22, 1849

French garden implements from the early nineteenth century, probably similar to the tools of Louisiana gardeners.

Charles Bailly, *Manuel complet théorique* (1825). Photograph courtesy of Dumbarton Oaks Garden Library.

to North America, which translated the tenets of the romantic English landscape movement to fit American conditions.

Downing made only a small impact in Louisiana, where most gardeners continued to adhere to the formal, geometric principles that had guided Le Nôtre in seventeenth-century France, if not to earlier, simpler geometric models. France had followed English taste toward freer forms, but southerners, particularly Louisianians, seemed to prefer the more orderly and controlled. That was so not only in the region of French heritage but also on plantations of English-speaking settlers. The notable exception to the preference for the formal was the garden of Valcour Aime, near Vacherie, in St. James Parish.

The *retardataire* attitudes toward garden design may have thrived because in relatively new and hostile country, the clearing and "taming" of a wild landscape required effort that made imitating nature seem contrary to immediate goals. The sectionalism that had begun to divide the country ideologically decades before the war may also have manifested itself in the Deep South's reluctance to join the trends in garden design that were evident in the North.

Far more can be discovered about the kinds of plants in ornamental gardens than about their arrangement in the gardens. Plant explorations and the importation of exotics from Asia during the late eighteenth and the early nineteenth century made a wide variety of ornamentals available. For many genera, there were more species available in the 1830s than a typical commercial nursery stocks today. Plants and seeds came by boat and rail. They were sometimes sold on the levee in New Orleans as soon as they arrived from abroad. Nurseries in New England also shipped plants to Louisiana, and regional nurseries supplied the trade as well. Plants were swapped with relatives and friends. They were propagated by cuttings, and they were transplanted. Family members living apart, especially a mother and her married daughters, exchanged plants almost as often as they wrote to each other. The mother's garden was frequently the source of many of the plants the daughter needed for an ornamental garden at her new home.

The life of everyone on a

I send you by Fanny a box of verbenas and phlox also some hearts ease. There are five different varieties of verbena. . . . You will also find five different varieties of the sweet pea.

—Allie Weeks Meade to Mary Clara Moore, April 2, 1857

plantation, whether planter, wife, child, or slave, was touched by the cultivation of gardens. The gardens were as important to some planters and their wives as the cash crops in the fields. No wide separation was apparent to them between the cultivation of the cotton and sugarcane and the tending of the camellias and China trees. The same weather and growing conditions that meant success or failure for the crops determined whether the kitchen garden and orchard would produce. The slave labor force that raised the crops was largely the same as the one that performed the heavy labor in establishing and maintaining ornamental gardens and landscapes. With the abolition of slavery, economies of scale ceased to exist for the large planter, and he and his family were no longer in a position to maintain pleasure grounds. The survival of nineteenth-century plantation gardens into the twentieth century was to a considerable degree the result of the sudden reduction in capital and labor. Planters and their wives could no longer afford to keep their gardens in step with changes in fashion.

VICTORIAN VESTIGES

Sometimes, through the portal, you catch a glimpse of a delicious garden, filled with daintiest blossoms, purple and white and red gleaming from the vines climbing over a gray wall; rose-bushes, with the grass about them strewn with loveliest petals; symmetrical green bouquets, and luxuriant hedges, arbors, and refuges, trimmed by skillful hands; banks of verbenas; bewitching profusion of peach and apple blossoms; dark green of the magnolia. . . . and a mass of rich bloom which laps the senses in slumbrous delight.

—Edward King, "Old and New Louisiana,"
Scribner's Monthly Magazine (1873)

The main boulevards of the city of New Orleans are all planted and well shaded with trees, and are perfectly delightful promenades. . . . They are studded with detached villas, great and small all surrounded by pretty gardens and a variety of tropical shrubs, also bananas and oranges. This profusion of gardens and flowers constitutes the great beauty of New Orleans.

—Maria Theresa Longworth, *Teresina in America* (1875)

With the onset of the Civil War, many men left home to fight for the Confederacy, and others went west in exile to wait out the conflict. Women were left with their homesteads and struggled to keep their families, slaves, and livestock fed and healthy. Although the war changed life in Louisiana, gardening remained "half of life," if not more. Cultivation of the kitchen garden and orchard was more critical than ever as access to markets became difficult and then impossible. Those plantations that Union troops had occupied for any length of time suffered destruction after fences were knocked down to get wood for camp fires. Without fences it was impossible to keep roaming animals out of the gardens.

Few Louisiana gardens from the war and postwar periods survive intact, yet it is possible to gain some idea of how important gardening remained during those years. Plantation gardens of the postbellum era have not commanded a great deal of scholarly attention, since the assumption has been that after the Civil War, people had neither the funds nor the "spirit" to change and "modernize" their domestic landscapes. But family correspondence and the black-and-white photographs that had become commonplace by 1870 suggest that gardening remained a central part of life. Andrew D. Lytle's photographic portraits of downtown Baton Rouge residences show handsome yards, with gardens of evergreens behind wrought-iron or wooden picket fences. Because photographs of family groups were often posed in front of the house or in the garden, to take

advantage of natural light, albums of old photographs can amount to garden vignettes.

The Sanborn fire insurance map of 1891 for Baton Rouge also attests to a continued interest in ornamental gardening. It presents the grounds of the Garig residence, now Lafayette Park, as exhibiting an elaborate garden scheme, complete with arbored walkway and gazebo. Quite a few of the drawings in the New Orleans Notarial Archives of Garden District and Uptown gardens from the postwar period show a more open and neighborly outlook than is evident in the introspective and private courtyards of the antebellum French Quarter.

Louisiana created its own version of the Victorian style that had become fashionable for gardens along the eastern seaboard around midcentury. The kinds of garden ornamentation and plants

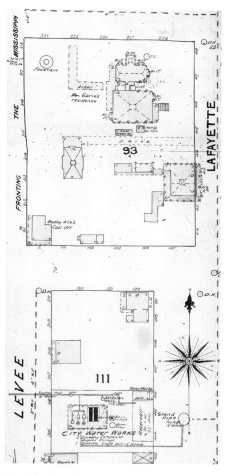

Two blocks in downtown Baton Rouge, as represented in Sanborn fire insurance maps, June, 1891. The elaborate residence of the Garig family, on the upper block, fronts the river, with circular fountain and L-shaped arbor between the house and the levee. The lower block was the site of the city waterworks and is today Lafayette Street Park.

Sanborn Map of Baton Rouge, Louisiana, 1891 (New York, 1891). Photograph courtesy of Louisiana and Lower Mississippi Valley Collections, LSU Libraries.

It is very pleasant to be at home, to think we do not have to be wanderers and exiles any more. . . . I have so much to employ me, trying to make a fall garden, which we need so much in these scarce times. I am planting, or rather have planted a large turnip patch, Irish potatoes, cabbage, lettuce, carrots, onions, beans, etc. & hope that I will have a good return from all that I have planted. We have not felt the need of a summer garden, as Mrs. Vaughn & Mrs. Richardson have supplied us most liberally everyday with vegetables and melons.

—Maggie Weeks to William Frederick Weeks, September 5, 1866

Family portrait in garden setting, probably in Baton Rouge. The shady side yard has a picket fence on one side and a board fence along the back. This outdoor room is furnished with urns, garden seats, and brick-bordered beds of aspidistras and other evergreens.

Andrew D. Lytle Album Photograph Collection, Louisiana and Lower Mississippi Valley Collections, LSU Libraries.

that are accorded the label Victorian certainly enjoyed a vogue in the South. The desirability of creating views from interior parlors and public rooms out to the landscape was accepted. Carpet bedding, that is, the composition of patterns on the ground with colorful annuals, and the use of exotic, subtropical foliage both appealed to Louisiana gardeners. But the highly controlled and manicured look that attended the style farther north was difficult to maintain under Louisiana's growing conditions, and the frustration of horticultural failure returned many short-lived ornamental beds to lawn. Instead, the state's gardeners had recourse to the evergreen palette, which was well suited to landscapes with mature shade trees. Large areas of full sun had become rare on residential properties by the turn of the century, and many gardens were under the canopy of a single live oak.

Faced with extensive gardens of vegetables and flowers but greatly reduced budgets for upkeep and virtually no labor force, planters had, at the least, to scale back their way of gardening. Often, however, they had to change their way of life completely. Rural properties might be boarded up or left in the hands of caretakers when the family moved to the city, where they could start anew in a different livelihood and buy a small piece of suburbia, if they were fortunate enough to be able to afford it. Often they brought cuttings and transplants to their young gardens from the plantations, sustaining a tenuous connection with home.

Martha Turnbull described in her diary her life as a widow trying to realize enough income from cotton to feed those dependent on her and to maintain the grandeur of her formal gardens. Her entries after the war were as specific as earlier, but she struck a new note of financial anxiety. In March, 1872, she sounded optimistically in tune with the change of seasons: "Everything putting out—looks like spring & flower garden & Yard look like old times, vegetable garden beautiful prospect. My garden by Extra help has cost me $85 up $2 to this time." A month later, she chronicled seasonal chores: "Clear today, plowing but wet. Mary & Fred, Augustus spaded up the Parterre, Greenhouse plants taken to the Avenue to be repotted. I have fifty little chickens. Augustus worked for two days for himself & Ben in pleasure ground cleaning Statues. Hawling trash from Avenue to clean and polish it up. Finished repotting Plants. Fixed Grave Yard today for the first time this year."

Turnbull had retained some of her former slaves as paid laborers and was struggling to eke out a living and have time for the horticultural pursuits that gave her most pleasure. She had a "truck patch," where she grew produce for market. Perhaps her greatest pride came from the propagation of camellias—the japonicas, as she called them. In March, 1874, Mr. Wilcox, a gardener, had "engrafted" some japonicas. A few days later she "put out 13 Japonicas that were in pots for the past 2 years." The following April Mr. Wilcox "put out 13 Japonicas of superior kinds."

For the Weeks family at Shadows-on-the-Teche, the situation after the war was even worse. Union troops had occupied the property, set up headquarters on the ground floor of the house, destroyed much of the fencing, and trampled the garden with their tents and horses. Mary Clara Weeks Moore, the mistress of the plantation, and the inspiration behind its gardens, had died in the house in 1864, during the Union occupation, and was buried on the property. Her son and daughter-in-law moved into the house and attempted to restore order to the landscape. Their daughter Lily had gardened at the feet of her mother and her grandmother and carried a love for flowers into her marriage to a New Orleans attorney, Gilbert Hall. Their ten-year courtship, which Gilbert's letters to Lily let us observe, included gifts of flowers and fruit sent by train from New Orleans to New Iberia or from New Iberia to New Orleans. In February, 1887, Gilbert wrote, "I send a list of choicest varieties of chrysanthemums selected at Maitre. They should be set out about the middle of March I understand. The catalogue that you desired I sent you as soon as it was printed by Maitre." The following month, Gilbert described the coming of spring to New Orleans: "The yards are lovely with beautiful flowers uptown now, and I know yours must be charming." Gilbert and Lily's only child, William Weeks Hall, inherited his parents' passion for gardening and eventually reclaimed the Shadows' gardens for himself and for posterity.

At The Cottage plantation, where Judge Thomas Butler and his wife, Anna, made their home in West Feliciana Parish, Anna continued tending her flowers and vegetables until her death in 1902. Three years before, when she was seventy-four years old, she had written to her daughter,

I have worked the strawberries in my garden, which look very well, and Edmund made Richmond set out in the old garden a great many plants left over from my bed. It will take days to cut away all of the dead branches on roses and shrubs and I am so thankful to feel well and be able to be out everyday. I hope your plants from Ellivay's have arrived, also the plants from Gauge & Co. I send you by Mim a root of the old flag, which I found in the old garden. You can divide it into three and when it blooms it will remind you of the days when you were running around here, and gathering the blue and white ones.

A visitor to The Cottage today may see only the dense vine-covered trees of the forest surrounding the plantation house, but Anna Butler's lifelong commentary on her gardening there is a reminder that the lush growth and shadow lie over a much-loved and carefully tended garden.

In the last quarter of the nineteenth century, as the South recalibrated its economy, shifting from agriculture to a more diversified base, the urbanized population no longer had to grow their own vegetables in order to put fresh food on the table. But ornamentals were no less appreciated, and as rail transport penetrated everywhere with swift service, gardeners ordered more and more plants through the mail, in order to have different and improved varieties with which to experiment. The way was gradually opening to a new prosperity in the succeeding century, when giving gardens pride of place would again be financially feasible both for those dwelling in privilege and for the average urban or suburban resident.

INTO THE TWENTIETH CENTURY: REVIVALISM AND THE AGE OF ESTATE GARDENS

The violet dusk held in soft suspension lights slow as bell strokes, Jackson Square was now a green and quiet lake . . . with silver mimosa and pomegranate and hibiscus beneath which lantana and cannas bled and bled. Pontalba and cathedral were cut from black paper and pasted flat on a green sky; above them taller palms were fixed in black and soundless explosions.

—William Faulkner, *Mosquitoes* (1927)

I'm very anxious to see what you are doing. Your ideas sound absolutely right—after all things that are typical are always the most interesting in any locality—and so few people seem to have any sense of restraint and balance in planting.

—F. Furness, Media, Pennsylvania, to William Weeks Hall, 1928

So sorry to hear of your accident and I hope this finds you in condition for spring gardening. Just got back from South America via freighter, which I really enjoyed. Saw plants which I would have given much to bring back—and which I think would thrive here—but I suppose that would take a Ned McIlhenny.

—Steele Burden to William Weeks Hall, *ca.* 1935

The industrial magnates on the eastern seaboard and in the Midwest ushered in a new era of garden building as their wealth allowed them to escape the cities' crowds and blight and retreat to the country. American capitalists, availing themselves of their enormous fortunes and the mobility that the innovation of the automobile afforded, were able to move their homes farther from the cities into scenic rural settings. Enclaves of country places sprang up on Long Island, in the Hudson River Valley, and in other places of natural beauty, most of them near water. The design of most of the estates, house and garden alike, harked back to the classical and traditional.

In American landscape history, the period from roughly 1880 to 1920 is sometimes called the Country Place Era, or the Golden Age, and the garden design of those years is typified by a concern for detail, the clear delineation of outdoor rooms, a restraint in plant selection, with primary reliance on architectonic evergreens, and an overall ethos of understatement. Attention usually focuses on the nationally known grand estates of the time—Biltmore, in North Carolina, one of the last designs of Frederick Law Olmsted; estates designed by Charles Platt; and Dumbarton Oaks, in Washington, D.C., designed by Beatrix Jones Farrand. Certainly the South did not produce magnates as prominent as the Rockefellers and the Du Ponts, but the discovery of oil along the Gulf Coast in 1901, together with booms in lumber and sugarcane, led to the ascendancy of a small group of millionaires, whose estates merit greater scholarly notice than they have received.

Architecture, garden design, furniture design, and the decorative arts were the uncontroversial, nonpolitical survivors of the antebellum period, owing to their extremely high quality and unique adaptation to the regional climate and building materials. Southerners took pride in the rich heritage from their own golden age and, in the optimism of the new century, intensified their efforts to ensure its survival.

By the second decade, investment, industrialization, and booming real estate had begotten a new generation of Louisiana gentry apt to seek possibilities for themselves in the places that had symbolized wealth and prosperity a century earlier: the plantations. Hundreds of big houses and their overgrown gardens dotted south Louisiana, and people responsive to the quality of the architecture, the beauty of the scenery, the privacy of the location, or the nostalgia of bygone days began to purchase these ghosts and breathe new life into them. The photographs of Clarence John Laughlin and Walker Evans capture poignantly the now-fabled deterioration of many of the great houses and their landscapes—a large number of which have long since disappeared. In most cases, the buyers of plantation sites gave much more attention and care to the buildings than to the landscape. Southerners of new wealth but no ancestral home often treated their new dwellings with the same reverence they would have shown if their forebears had lived there.

Notwithstanding the widespread impression of the provincialism of the South in the first half of the twentieth century and of the conservatism that encumbered most aspects of society and politics, southerners of means then, as always, put great value on staying up-to-date with intellectual and aesthetic as well as political and cultural trends, both nationally and internationally. Before the Civil War, planters from along the Gulf Coast were frequent visitors to the economic and cultural centers of New York and Philadelphia, and there was very little lag in the transfer of East Coast ideas and styles to the Deep South. Among the wealthy families of the South, there was a sophistication much at odds with southern stereotypes. During the early decades of the twentieth century, part of the education of the children of the gentry was training in the arts, particularly music or painting. After mastering the basics of the art form, young adults could expect to be favored with a study tour of Europe as part of their rite of passage. Technology seemed to be driving the future of the United States, and Europe seemed the preserve of intellectual and artistic innovation. In 1907, the first cubist painting exhibition was held in Paris, and in 1908 the first steel-and-glass building was constructed in Berlin. Although impressionism had revolutionized the way the artist saw the world in the last century, by 1910 the abstraction and reduction of the landscape and the human form were the preoccupation of the European avant-garde.

By contrast, American architects and garden designers were looking back rather than ahead. The 1913 New York Armory Show introduced postimpressionism and cubism to America, shocking the artistic establishment. In the same year, the publication of a monograph of Platt's architectural and landscape designs left a lasting mark on the American design community. Platt had first gained recognition for his *Italian Gardens* (1894), the first book in English on Italian Renaissance gardens. Platt, as a student of painting, had felt the effects of his own sojourn in Europe, and upon his return he had turned to architecture and garden design, becoming one of the leading designers of country houses and gardens in the nation. *Italian Gardens* introduced American architects and landscape designers to the ideal of the Italian villa, where house and garden are conceived as a single entity, a sequence of connected indoor and outdoor rooms. According to Platt, Italian models might be useful for a "more thorough understanding and appreciation for the reasons which led to a formal treatment of the garden; and as there is a great similarity in the character of the landscape in many parts of our country with that of Italy, . . . it might lead to a revival of the same method." Platt struck a responsive chord in the United States with his persuasive promotion of architectonic formal gardens.

At the turn of the century, there were in America both formal and natural schools of garden design. In England, William Robinson reacted against the artificiality and excesses of late Victorian carpet bedding by espousing the alternative of naturalized layouts and hardy native and hardy and half-hardy exotic varieties. Although the American landscape architect Jens Jensen designed a "prairie river" for the Chicago park system and attempted to re-create native prairie vegetation in many of his estate designs, the majority of practicing landscape designers of the time did not follow his lead. It was not until the 1970s that the exclusive use of native species and the scientific re-creation of habitats and plant communities were to become a live option in popular design and bring an aesthetic of ecology to the fore.

Like Platt, William Weeks Hall spent time studying painting abroad and acquired a predilection for classical landscape design as a result. After his father's death, Hall had gone to the Pennsylvania Academy of the Fine Arts, where he won the traveling scholarship that permitted his extended European tour. Before setting sail, in 1919, Hall decided that he would rescue his ancestral home, Shadows-on-the-Teche, when he returned. Writing to a friend in 1921, he described his encounters with some of the artistic giants working then, and we almost see Hall grow in his awareness of the broader implications art can have for society:

I haven't been doing much work, as Paris hasn't impressed me very favourably and is in dozens of ways so very far behind the times. The present French taste is execrable and the arrangement of exhibitions and the interior decoration is rotten. I found the schools and exhibitions in England a great deal better, and as far as the clothes, leather goods, and theaters are concerned, I would like to live there a long time. The attitude in England, too, is rather more trusting than the French, who . . . regard the American quite as he does the German unless he comes from the office of Pierpont Morgan or is related to the Rothschilds.

Of course, the average tourist and the artist likes the picturesque, but that, as a word, has no definition for me. The whole of the French life seems consecrated to the senses rather than to an intellectual problem. . . . The consequence is, I doubt if there is a man with French blood in his veins who is today painting great pictures.

I saw in his garden, the great Monet. He came down to his gate and looked at me as though he wanted to throw me in his cheap little lily pond, of which he is now painting, a very vigorous man at the age of eighty-two, ten decorations to be given to the French government. Can you imagine a lily pond as he paints it, decorating anything?

I have seen a very great exhibition by a very intellectual and thoughtful painter, as a Spanish painter can sometimes be. I don't think you'd like him right away. I didn't, but after two years, I have the greatest admiration in a very careful way, even for his cubist things, though I don't quite get them. His other things are completely devoid of Gallic excitement, and some day I'm going to write him and see if I can't meet him, though I have been offered a direct introduction already. Pablo Picasso.

The things that Matisse did in Nice this winter prove him to be an absolute faker, and I don't think that he has ever been able to do anything. The Salon was the most horrible thing I have ever seen and bears no relation to the sort of thing there must have been fifty years ago. The schools here are simply vile, and England and Germany both are far in advance, I am sorry to say.

In 1922, Hall wrote to his cousin Ned,

My trip has not been very fruitful and I haven't enjoyed it at all in the degree which I expected. I find things still suffering from the mental attitude of such a great catastrophe as the last unpleasantness. . . . I have been to London, to Holland, to Belgium, back to Paris, to Chartres, Angers, and last week down to Poitiers. At this last place, full of marvelous twelfth and fifteenth century remains, and even a building dating from 300 A.D., I found a great deal to interest me. . . .

I have been struck very much by the similarity in temperament and customs in the French provincial towns to the Creoles around home; the same characteristics seem implanted throughout generations, and the only thing that we lack is the beautiful surroundings that the French countryside usually possesses. I had intended to go to Italy, but I don't think I will.

Hall's exposure to the historic architecture of Europe and the tradition of preservation made an impression. As he traveled, he seems to have been thinking of his own heritage and developing a deeper awareness of its roots and its value. While still abroad, Hall sent instructions to his architect, Richard Koch, who had himself studied in Paris, and to his caretaker at the Shadows, coordinating the first stages of restoration of his homeplace.

In 1922 and 1923, Hall began to reestablish the ornamental landscape there, building on the "bones" of his grandmother's and great-grandmother's gardens and creating a series of garden rooms that recalled the refinement of antebellum plantations. As part of planning his personal garden, he had visited many of the old plantation grounds along the Mississippi River, including Rosedown, in St. Francisville. By his testimony, he had attempted to design a garden compatible with the 1830s mansion that was the centerpiece of the Shadows.

His garden was one of the earliest in the region for which there was a conscious intention to revive the mood and feeling of the southern plantation garden, and it influenced the design of many others in the area. The landscape designs by Steele Burden, of Baton Rouge, over a sixty-year career carry the imprint of Hall's approach, which involved the use of sculpture and garden ornaments to set focal points, shade-tolerant evergreens to define garden rooms, and subtropical and tropical perennials to introduce seasonal interest and texture.

While transformations were under way on plantations, some who could afford living in style were acting on their preference for

Shadows-on-the-Teche, side garden designed by William Weeks Hall in the 1920s. Camellias planted by Hall's grandmother form the centerpiece to the garden. A row of antique olive jars is the backdrop for a planting bed at the right.
Photograph by I. A. Martin, 1930s, Collection of Shadows-on-the-Teche

the suburban estate. In 1935, the Edgar Stern family, of New Orleans, engaged Ellen Biddle Shipman, a respected landscape designer from the East who had trained with Platt, to lay out the grounds around their modest house. Once they began thinking about the new garden with its axial vistas, however, the Sterns decided that their house did not measure up to the grandeur of the setting. Shipman recommended Platt's sons William and Geoffrey as architects for a new house. Longue Vue, as the Stern estate became known, achieved distinction not only for its landscape but also for its Classical Revival mansion, inspired by earlier architecture in Louisiana. One facade of Longue Vue was based on a facade of Shadows-on-the-Teche.

The Sterns and Hall were friends, and Edith Stern often wrote and asked Hall's advice about plants for her gardens. When Shipman came to New Orleans to lecture, in 1934, Edith Stern had tried to persuade Hall to meet her. But Hall was a recluse and declined. Resolute, Shipman went to New Iberia anyway. She was able to tour Hall's garden, but he did not meet her.

Hall lived within a few miles of the McIlhenny nursery, at Avery Island, then one of the largest and most successful commercial growers in the region. Hall bought many of his plants, including camellias, azaleas, and bamboo, from the nursery and was a friend of its proprietor, Edward Avery McIlhenny, often corresponding on horticultural questions and asking advice on the choice of plants. The McIlhenny nursery supplied the plants for Huey Long's new state capitol, and an employee may even have designed the gardens. Burden was a frequent customer, buying plants for the LSU campus when it was under construction, in the 1930s. The Shadows was a regular stop on Burden's trip to Avery Island, since he and Hall were well acquainted.

In 1922, Mathilda Gray, a native of Lake Charles, who had inherited a great deal of money that had been made in oil, as well as valuable land, built a family estate in her hometown. Gray developed elaborate theme gardens around her mansion, including an oriental garden. She also rescued Evergreen, a plantation on the west side of the Mississippi between Baton Rouge and New Orleans. She restored and modernized the big house and also saved an outstanding collection of dependencies and slave quarters.

Although a small group of Americans amassed great fortunes, the great majority were less positively affected by changes in the national economy after World War I. The federal Works Progress Administration (WPA), which gave hope to a nation in severe economic depression, also contributed to the preservation of the Louisiana plantation landscape. Under its aegis, the Historic American Buildings Survey hired unemployed architects and draftsmen in the 1930s to document architectural masterworks of the nineteenth century in measured drawings and photographs.

The WPA also provided funding for the improvement of public parks. City Park, in New Orleans, is what it is today because of this program. The gardens in the park are of a design that has persisted to the present in south Louisiana landscapes, with a reliance on evergreens for the greater part of a planting and heavy use of ground covers and bordering plants like liriope, mondo grass, and aspidistra. Flowering evergreen shrubs, such as azaleas and camellias, provide seasonal interest. Only the formal rose garden in the center of City Park departs from the informal picturesque character of the rest of the grounds. That garden, today the New Orleans Botanical Garden, addressed the desperate yearning that the urban populace had for a connection with a cultivated landscape. It provided the public with something on the scale of a residential landscape, where they could come with their families, stroll, and reconnect through flowers, their fragrance, and the beauty of ordered nature.

Those who were able to maintain their ownership of suburban properties through the depression continued to garden. Their gardens tended to be rectilinear, often taking form from the dimensions of the lot. Smaller outdoor rooms were created, extending from the sides of the residence; often ornamental sculptures or fountains provided an axial focus. Annuals, roses, and flowering plants requiring full sunlight were used sparingly or not at all.

AT MIDCENTURY: PRIVATE GARDENS AS PUBLIC PLACES

The American Bicentennial brought with it not only a renewed emphasis on the American heritage but also the beginning of a serious recognition that landscapes are a component of the heritage. Institutions private and public began making hard decisions about preserving notable landscapes of the American past and ensuring their accessibility to the public.

One reaction was to convert private estates into public institutions, sometimes combining a house museum and display gardens. Longue Vue, ELsong, and Zemurray gardens, as well as the Shadows, are now operated by organizations that open them to the public. No longer does a family or a single owner control each garden's care and evolution. The garden as an emblem of an individual's creative vision has been replaced by consensus building and budgeting. The intimacy between garden and gardener has changed.

Hall realized as a young man with no heirs that his wish for the Shadows was that the next generations of Louisianians might be able to see it and appreciate the beauty of its design. He denied the city of New Iberia's request to purchase it as a park and recreation center; he foresaw how that would compromise the property's historical integrity. He preferred to leave his family place to a public institution capable of ensuring that it would endure as he had known it. It took him over a decade to make arrangements that included all the protections he wanted. He prepared two notebooks setting out the history of the house and gardens, his intentions for them, and directions for maintenance. Unlike gardens where the link to the garden maker is lost, the Shadows today communicates to the visitor an impression of four generations of a Louisiana family and how they lived and gardened in their landscape.

The public's response has served to confirm that as a nation we desire to have access to beautifully designed landscapes, to participate in the marriage of art and nature. More and more of us are consequently looking to our own settings, regardless of how small and transient, in the hope of a fuller participation. The fervor to garden has never been stronger in Louisiana, a state where life has always been inseparable from cultivation and the soil. It is up to us to choose whether we will continue in dialogue with the landscape, whether we will make the effort to discover places the past of which has not yet been unlocked or celebrated, and whether we will commit ourselves to the preservation of green places where we can be reminded of who we are as a culture, and where we came from.

LOOKING BACK TO LOOK AHEAD: THE GARDEN OF VALCOUR AIME

The old order has to die before there can be a born-again landscape. Many of us know the joy and excitement not so much of creating the new as of redeeming what has been neglected, and this excitement is particularly strong

The salient garden trend of the final quarter of the twentieth century has been the movement to preserve old gardens, and in our new gardens to recall aspects of the old. Agencies public and private are hiring professionals to assist in the preservation of historic gardens. A body of literature has accumulated that explains techniques of garden preservation. An entire industry has arisen to provide the plants and furnishings for historic landscapes. So what next? And why are we doing this in the first place?

What is the future of the garden as an idea and as a place? Just as the lawn mower, the automobile, and modern herbicides dramatically altered the ways we garden, surely change will continue at a rapid pace. The faster change sweeps through our culture, the harder we will hold to our images of the past. Our motive will be security, as well as reverence and respect for a time and place that somehow seem to make sense.

The story behind the garden of Valcour Aime catches our individual and collective fascination with the garden as a mythical ideal. That garden today is a virtual ruin. After Aime abandoned it in 1854, after the weakness of the postbellum economy took its toll, and after nature had its way for a half century, people began to visit the garden. The fences had long since rotted, and only a strand or two of barbed wire protected the heart of the garden from the outside world. First, the ornaments of the garden had been removed: sculptures of the four seasons now adorn a rural church courtyard, the plantation bell is on exhibit at a museum, the gates were reinstalled at a modern mansion, the fountainhead graces a private courtyard pool. Well-intended plantsmen, wishing to rescue Aime's prized exotics from the competition of natural vegetative succession, removed most of the ornamentals and took them to the safety of their own gardens. Plants assumed the name of the garden from which they hailed: there is a Valcour Aime mahonia, for example, a Valcour

Aime bamboo, and roses supposedly propagated from cuttings obtained in the garden. Soon the only plants left were the trees forming the dense canopy, and the seasonal ground covers and perennials that will come back eternally in south Louisiana.

The more people who visited the garden, the easier it became to maneuver through the undergrowth, and paths were discovered and reopened. The garden informally became a public park of sorts—

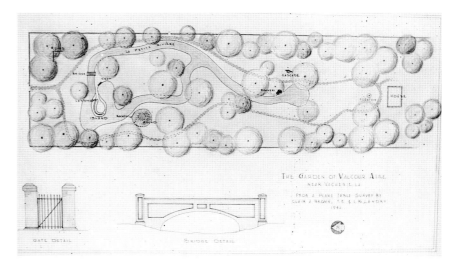

A Preliminary Sketch of the Garden of Valcour Aime, by Clair A. Brown and Theodore E. Landry, 1941. This scale drawing constitutes the most comprehensive documentation available of the gardens as they existed earlier in the twentieth century.

Photograph of the plantation house of Valcour Aime, showing Chinese bridge in the foreground. Although much of the garden survives in a ruined state, the house and this bridge have been destroyed.

a place for people to hike and stroll, a place for children to explore and climb, a place for teenagers to hide, a place for college students to take dates. As people made use of the garden, they stumbled upon artifacts—a piece of ceramic, the head of a broken porcelain doll, a small crucifix, the blade of a gardening tool. Their finders took such treasures of magical discovery home, keepsakes and reminders of a place not of their time.

Guides led tourists and garden connoisseurs, sharing the story and the mystery of the place with visitors prepared to brave the mosquitoes. A fraternity of sorts grew up of those who had descended from Aime and those who had been touched by his garden—a doctor in Texas, a geographer in Canada, a priest in Lafayette. Recently some of those who cherish the garden and are anxious to ensure its future met in it to share their stories and plan for the future.

The future of this garden is still unsettled. Today an aluminum fence protects it from destruction by dirt bikes. After surviving nearly a century and a half in ruins, a portion of the wall of the mock fortress fell to such motorcycles. A camera crew carrying heavy equipment to shoot footage for a documentary overstressed one of the footbridges, and it collapsed. An archaeologist from California learned that Aime and the pirate Jean Laffite were friends and has concluded that Laffite's long-lost treasure may be buried on the site. He wants to probe and electronically scan the garden.

How can a ten-acre garden have occasioned all this? Why does Aime loom larger than life? What about this dark and wooded place attracts such a following?

For one thing, there has been an ample record of Aime's remarkable life and labors in St. James Parish. The publication of translated excerpts of Aime's plantation diary by his grandson in 1878 gave access to Aime's own account of his life. The complete translation of his diary by the WPA, with marginal notations, expanded the story and made it available in libraries nationwide. Writers of popular histories and historical novelists had a field day with Aime's story, embellishing it shamelessly. Typescripts of the journal that

Gabriel, Aime's son, kept while traveling in Europe during the years before his death have been photocopied and passed along to those following the story.

Perhaps the passion with which Aime lived, pursuing success as a planter, as a horticulturist, and as a connoisseur of garden design, had something to do with the legend. Perhaps it was the poignant story of the man whose life was finished by the death of his only son. More likely, it was the power of the place, the garden itself, that ensured Le Petit Versailles a place in the history of Louisiana gardening. To walk through this landscape is to experience secondhand the thick Louisiana "jungle" that the earliest explorers encountered. To see the rivulet the hands of hundreds of slaves excavated from swampland is to begin to imagine the enormous scale of this experiment in settlement. To come upon the faux rockworks forming the foundations of a fortress folly or the exquisite brick arch in the remains of a footbridge is to be reminded of the sophistication and craftsmanship that came to the wilderness early on. To discover the mound deep within the garden and to enter the opening and look up and see a brick corbeled dome is to recognize the mindset of the planter class that, despite the isolation of plantations, insisted on creating small pieces of culture and whimsy. And to see the size of the trunks of the great magnolias and live oaks is to be struck by the force of time and nature in this place where temperature and humidity create a virtual greenhouse for the trees of the forest.

What speaks to the visitor to Aime's garden is one man's personal vision and deep attachment to a place. It is a message that is harder to hear in strolling manicured paths of a restored garden where signs identifying genus and species mediate between seasonal color and the viewer. What Aime's garden offers is the possibility to experience a place, not to be processed through it.

What are the implications if a ruin means more than a beautiful restoration? What does that suggest we are looking for in a garden today? The answers, though not clear, matter a great deal.

Garden Profiles

URBAN BEGINNINGS

Away we rattled through narrow dirty streets, among grimy old stuccoed walls; high, arched windows and doors, balconies and entresols, and French noises and French smells (nothing so strong, in association, as old smells); French signs, ten to one of English. . . .

I was delighted when I reached the old Place d'Armes, now a public garden, bright with orange and lemon trees, and roses, and myrtles, and laurels, and jessamines of the south of France. . . .

First and last, I spent some weeks in New Orleans and its vicinity. I doubt if there is a city in the world, where the resident population has been so divided in its origin, or where there is such a variety in the tastes, habits, manners, and moral codes of the citizens.

—Frederick Law Olmsted, *A Journey in the Seaboard Slave States* (1856)

Hermann-Grima House
820 St. Louis Street
New Orleans French Quarter

When Samuel Hermann purchased the large tract of property bounded by St. Louis, Bourbon, Dauphine, and Conti Streets in 1823, the site had already been through a generation or two of development and habitation. Hermann eventually demolished the existing house, presumably a smaller and simpler structure than the Georgian town house and courtyard complex he made plans with his architect to construct, as suiting a merchant of his stature. In 1831, at the time of construction, the yard behind the old house had been paved with brick laid in a herringbone pattern. Hermann selected the more durable flagstone that came as ship ballast from Europe and had it laid directly atop the brick. Archaeology has revealed the location of a well immediately behind the old house but has been unable to make out much more about the configuration of that building's site.

Hermann's complex was at the time one of the largest holdings in the French Quarter and adapted to the necessities of a densely populated, highly urbanized setting. Although the merchant was of German descent, he built according to the conventions of the French, positioning the house directly against the sidewalk, or banquette, and reserving the rest of the lot as an enclosed private space. In the 1830s, the streets of the French Quarter were not the scenic passageways they are today. Instead, they were often wet and muddy, impassable in heavy rain. Ditches alongside the banquettes carried all forms of refuse, from dead animals and household garbage to night soil. But messy and unsanitary conditions did not spare the streets from heavy use. Horse-drawn carriages traversed the neighborhood, and vendors and peddlers carried goods from the levees and French Market into the residential sectors. The streets were also the domain of the kind of street life that any port of call attracts, with sailors, vagrants, and other threatening types abounding. The walled court of the typical French Quarter residence provided protection and psychological separation from the chaos outside. Behind the walls, most of what took place had to do with the daily tasks of life in the city. The court was the only outdoor space for the use of the slaves and their families and for the gentry living in the town house. House servants lived in dependencies like the three-story detached wing on the Hermann-Grima parcel. In the climate of New Orleans, outdoor space was not a luxury. Surviving the tropical summer temperatures and high humidity depended on it. Cross ventilation went only so far in relieving the oppressiveness of the heat.

In the courtyard, people could go about their business in a modicum of comfort conferred by the occasional shade of a tree and the soothing movement of breezes.

The Hermann-Grima courtyard is still laid out as it was in 1831. The long narrow raised planting beds were typical of the time and place and probably constituted a simplified local version of the parterre beds favored in French courtyard and garden design. The beds were slightly raised to provide drainage, since the city was below sea level, the soil saturated, and the water table very high. Surprisingly, the arrangement of the raised beds in this court does not match the high style of the house, with its formal central hall—a legacy of the architecture of the Federalized eastern seaboard—and its symmetrically flanking paired suites of rooms. The beds are not of equal width and do not relate to the central axis of the house.

The kitchen, storage rooms, and ironing room open onto the court, so that the work conducted in the rooms spilled out into the court. An adjacent courtyard housed the stables. The luxuriant planting and inviting brick patio there today replace a horse yard crowded with hay and equipment. The stable is now a gift shop, but the stalls and hay troughs remain to remind the visitor of its original function.

Not much is known about the planting of French Quarter courtyards during the first half of the nineteenth century. Most travelers' accounts mention hedges or orchards of orange trees as one of their first impressions of the city and region, and today the Hermann-Grima beds are largely planted with kumquats, the hardiest citrus. Several volunteer trees from after the Civil War, when the upkeep of properties lagged, shade the back beds, rendering out of the question the sun-loving plants that originally filled them. Shrubs, roses, and subtropical perennials dating from the nineteenth century, particularly varieties with a pronounced fragrance, occupy the remainder of the beds.

Kumquats in courtyard, kitchen on right

Dead banana branch

Angel trumpet blossoms

Kumquats, looking toward kitchen

Courtyard and back of house

Beauregard-Keyes House
1113 Chartres Street
New Orleans French Quarter

What is now known as the Beauregard-Keyes house was built across from the Ursuline Convent in 1826, and seven years later became the home of the Swiss consul, John A. Merle. It was during Merle's ownership that the large garden was constructed. The immense size is extremely unusual for this period in the French Quarter, when most makers of formal residential gardens adjusted to the constriction of town lot sizes by fashioning long, narrow garden rooms.

The house and its garden were measured for the New Orleans Notarial Archives in 1865, and the parterre of the present day is a reconstruction based on archival plans, but slightly smaller. Behind the house is a more typical small courtyard, probably originally the work yard for the residence and the location of detached dependencies.

Much of the site's renown, and in any case its name, owes to the two most celebrated residents of the house. In 1865, at the end of the Civil War, when the Confederate general Pierre G. T. Beauregard returned home to New Orleans, he lodged in the house for eighteen months. In 1925, after plans were announced to demolish the house and build a macaroni factory, a group of patriotic women rallied to its rescue, raising funds to save it.

In 1944, the novelist Frances Parkinson Keyes came to Louisiana, rented the house, and then took it over and began its restoration. It was under Keyes's stewardship that the formal garden was reconstructed. The house was her winter home for a quarter century, and she wrote several of her novels in residence. In 1948, the Keyes Foundation was formed, and today the house and garden are open to the public under its sponsorship.

Fountain and parterre

Snowdrops in parterre

St. Francis

Roots

Oak trunk and sculpture

Courtyard with fountain

Plantation Gardens

For twenty miles to the north of the town, there is on both sides a succession of large sugar and cotton plantations. Much land still remains uncultivated, however. The roadside fences are generally hedges of roses—Cherokee and sweet brier. These are planted first by the side of a common rail fence, which, while they are young, supports them in the manner of a trellis; as they grow older they fall each way, and mat together. . . . Trumpet creepers, grapevines, green-briers, and in very rich soil, cane, grow up through the mat of roses, and add to its strength.

There were frequent groves of magnolia grandiflora, large trees, and every one in the glory of full blossom. The large-leafed magnolia, extremely beautiful at this season of the year, was more rarely seen.

The plantation residences were of a cottage class, sometimes with extensive and tasteful grounds around them.

—Frederick Law Olmsted, *A Journey in the Back Country* (1860)

Parlange
New Roads

Among the oldest surviving structures in Louisiana, the Parlange plantation house was built at the end of the eighteenth century for the Marquis Vincent de Ternant. Descendants of the original owner still occupy it. The house fronts on False River, an oxbow lake formed when the Mississippi changed course in the geologic past. Originally the plantation's cash crop was indigo, but along with most of its lakefront counterparts, Parlange converted to sugarcane in the early 1800s. The plantation continued with that staple crop until recently.

The house is an excellent illustration of the principles of Creole architecture, with wide verandas completely surrounding it so as to provide what is essentially a second house in the cover and shade of the galleries. In this kind of house, life took place both inside and outside, with constant passage between the two. The galleries were large enough for family meals and daytime and overnight sleep during the summer months. Those on the second, or main, floor survey the landscape. The lake terminates the vista from the front gallery, and the cultivated fields stretch to the horizon at the back. Pecan orchards lie on both sides of the main yard.

Most visible from the road are the two white two-story *pigeon-niers* flanking the central entrance drive. Such outbuildings frequently functioned as ornamental gatehouses on French plantations of the period. But practically, too, the French settlers raised pigeons for the table and for their droppings, which make a rich fertilizer.

We can only imagine what the gardens at Parlange were like in the eighteenth and nineteenth centuries. Along with most of the French settling on that side of the river, the family would have wanted extensive kitchen gardens and orchards, as well as ornamental gardens. One very ancient live oak to the left of the house probably predates the building. An allée of cedars, rather than the more customary live oaks, lined the entrance drive. A few of them still stand, although a recent hurricane caused much damage.

The garden at Parlange today is the creation of Steele Burden dating from the 1950s. Occupying the area to the right of the house, it is an informal stroll garden punctuated by ornaments that include sculpture and fountains. The rich palette of shade-loving evergreens makes for a lush textural composition. A family pet cemetery, complete with markers, is along the path. A sugar-kettle fountain recalls the industry that built the family fortune many years ago.

Spanish moss and *pigeonnier*

The god Pan in sugar kettle

Pet cemetery

Rice-paper plants in bloom

Bronze figure and water plants

Classical bust and vines

Maison Chenal
Chenal

Too many of the surviving early gardens of Louisiana have ceased to receive the personal care of their makers and the descendants of their makers. With public ownership comes a certain distancing of a garden from the human relationships that originally defined its existence. A sterility at times creeps in with the systematic maintenance plans and the professional groundskeepers. At Maison Chenal, the garden, a recent creation of the property's owners, Jack and Pat Holden, bears the stamp of the kind of daily attention, in company with a love of plants and experimentation with horticultural specimens, that was the hallmark of our gardening forebears. The Holdens have devoted a great deal of their lives to the study of early Louisiana—its architecture, decorative arts, textiles, and gardens. Their collection of early Louisiana furniture is second to none, and for many years they have shared it with the Louisiana State Museum.

In 1975, the Holdens began assembling what is now known as Maison Chenal, moving an eighteenth-century Creole house from a nearby site to near the Chenal, a channel running from the Mississippi levee into False River. They began with the restoration and furnishing of the main house and then developed the garden surrounding the house.

Maison Chenal today affords one of the most complete pictures of life during the late eighteenth and the early nineteenth century in this Creole section of south Louisiana. The Holdens have with a sensitivity born of careful study added outbuildings, including an overseer's house, a loom house, pens and coops for chickens, ducks, and turkeys, a boathouse on the banks of the Chenal, and perhaps the most vivid rendition of an outside kitchen in the state. The kitchen building, moved from another location, feels as if hundreds of years of savory meals have smoked its timbers and warmed its dirt floors. Entering this building is as close to stepping back to an earlier Louisiana as it is possible to come.

The gardens of Maison Chenal are based on written and graphic evidence the Holdens amassed, including what is in drawings in the New Orleans Notarial Archives. The front entry garden consists of a geometric parterre of lozenge-shaped beds edged by privet. Seasonal flowers typical of the period add color. The garden's enclosing *pieux* fence is cloaked in antique roses. Behind the main house is the *potager*, or kitchen garden, with a central arbor covered with grape vines. In the raised rectangular beds with wooden frames, period vegetables, herbs, and flowers flourish.

Gate to guesthouse, with antique roses

Pigeonnier

Vegetable and flower garden with bell jar

View of front parterre from gallery

View of back garden from gallery

Aging Osage orange trunks

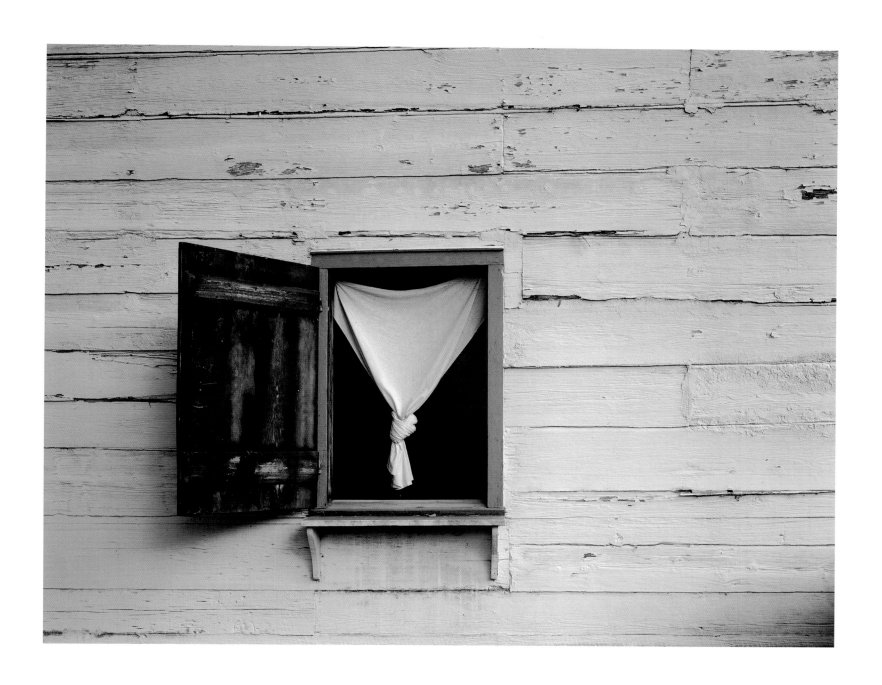

Kitchen window with knotted curtain

Entrance road looking across highway to guest cottage on banks of Chenal

L'Hermitage
Darrow

L'Hermitage plantation traces its origins to 1804, when Emmanuel Marius Pons Bringier purchased land for growing indigo. The first crop was harvested in 1807, and in 1811 ownership of the plantation was transferred to Bringier's son, Michel, who began constructing a house on the grounds soon after his marriage in 1812. The young couple moved in not long after the birth of their first child, in 1814. As a member of a militia, Bringier went on to fight under General Andrew Jackson in the Battle of New Orleans; he named the plantation after the general's home in Nashville. Jackson is supposed to have visited L'Hermitage twice, once with his wife, Rachel, and again in 1840 for the commemoration of the twenty-fifth anniversary of the battle.

Bringier was a successful planter, shifting his crop to sugarcane once the market for indigo declined and the health hazards that its processing incurred became widely known. He owned nearby Houmas plantation (32,000 acres) and Maison Blanche (2,500 acres). The Bringiers had ten children and eventually added a two-story wing to the rear of the main house to accommodate the family. This addition was removed in 1932 because of its poor condition.

In 1833, Bringier described L'Hermitage in his journal as consisting of the main house, two *pigeonniers,* a kitchen, a hospital, a smokehouse, a sugarhouse, storehouses, four barns, ten slave cabins, eighty slaves, and livestock. When he died of cancer, in 1847, his wife and one of their sons took over its operation.

The Civil War was damaging to the fortunes of the Bringiers. Union troops confiscated the property in 1863 and leased it to a carpetbagger from New England, James Baxter. When the Bringiers returned at the close of the war, they found the plantation badly maintained. They restored it to prosperity before selling it to Duncan F. Kenner, the husband of Nanine, one of the Bringier daughters. Kenner, of nearby Ashland plantation, owned L'Hermitage until his death, in 1887.

In 1911, a speculator and developer bought the property with the idea of transforming it into the city of St. Elmo. Although that project never came to reality, a plot plan dating from the period recorded all the outbuildings Bringier mentioned in his list in 1833, as well as a double row of oaks on each side of the central entry drive, and two double rows of pecans six hundred feet apart flanking the oak allée.

In 1959, Robert and Susan Judice, of New Orleans, rescued L'Hermitage plantation from neglect and desertion when they bought the house and twenty-five acres around it. By then, none of the outbuildings remained and the house was in serious disrepair.

The oak allée had been felled in 1919, but the downriver rows of pecan trees still recalled the formality of the earlier entrance planting between the house and the river. What gardens might have existed in the plantation's prosperous years were overgrown and indistinguishable. The Judices were dedicated to restoring and furnishing the big house authentically, and they moved outbuildings from nearby sites to create something comparable to the original complex adjacent to the house. They enlisted the services of Theodore and Lou Landry, of Port Allen, in redeveloping the landscape. The Landrys put a fenced yard around the house, with plantings of pyramidal cypresses along the front fence. On the downriver side of the house they laid out a rectangular garden room with a central grass panel and borders of small flowering trees and flowering herbaceous plants appropriate to the region and to the period of the house's construction. A summerhouse at the far end of this room constitutes a terminus of the axis and serves as a refuge from the glare of the summer sun. Gnarled trunks and sinuous branches of two ancient live oaks frame the view from the ground-floor gallery that looks out on this simple and elegant room.

The Judices added a brick patio behind the main house and an outbuilding beyond that to accommodate and feed tour groups. A guesthouse overlooking the rectangular side garden contributes to the effect of clustered buildings typical of a nineteenth-century sugar plantation. The Judices have continued to refine the landscape and in 1990 replanted the central allée of thirty-six live oaks, reinstating the formal entry drive for future generations.

PRIEST'S COTTAGE AND GARDEN

In 1979, Father Gerard Young, a Catholic priest, purchased land adjacent to the Judices' and originally part of the L'Hermitage tract for a personal retreat. He moved two historic houses from nearby plantations, one dating from 1790 and the other from the 1830s, and built a connecting hallway between them. Then he began to shape the landscape around a set of outbuildings and garden structures. By adding a wing and extensive front and back gardens, he has created a remarkably convincing illustration of the way the owner of a modest property would have lived and gardened in the nineteenth century.

Tree house, tree, and house

Front gallery

Front gate to priest's cottage, with recycled *pieux* fence

Wisteria arbor behind priest's cottage

Inner courtyard of priest's garden looking to front garden

Back of priest's garden, with pump and shrine

White wisteria

Houmas House
Burnside

The River Road between Baton Rouge and New Orleans summarizes the story of economic development in the region of the lower Mississippi Valley that it passes through. The pie-slice landholdings that once ran along the entire corridor are still discernible. But overlying the French pattern of long lots are petrochemical complexes of huge proportions. Clusters of ancient live oaks often mark the sites of the sugarcane plantations that exploited the fertility of the alluvial soil and included the first factories on the Mississippi. Sometimes only the oaks have survived to remind us of what used to be.

Near the town of Burnside, three great plantations stand together: L'Hermitage, Bocage, and Houmas House. All three retain their exquisite architectural and site integrity, because early preservationists of the area lavished care on them.

The land on which Houmas House sits was originally purchased from the Houmas Indians, and the small house at the rear of the great Greek Revival mansion known today as Houmas House was built in the last quarter of the eighteenth century. John and Caroline Preston, of Columbia, South Carolina, constructed the mansion in 1840. She was the daughter of the Revolutionary War hero General Wade Hampton, and the Hampton family held substantial

properties from Pennsylvania to Texas. Almost nothing is known about what the immediate grounds of Houmas House were like at first, but it is thought that there were elaborate ornamental gardens in front of the house. Behind the house was the working yard with its outbuildings and chicken coops.

In 1858, the planter John Burnside, an Irishman, purchased the plantation, and the Prestons returned to Columbia. Under Burnside's custody, it grew to twenty thousand acres, and four mills processed the sugarcane grown there. At its height, the plantation was the prime sugar producer in America.

In South Carolina, the Prestons built another house, Millwood, that Union troops set on fire. Recently a landscape plan for Houmas house has come to light among papers kept at a house the family had in town.

Houmas House was spared during the Civil War, with Burnside claiming personal immunity in virtue of being a British subject. Between his death, in 1881, and the turn of the century, the plantation had two more owners. When Colonel William Porcher Miles, a successful planter, died, most of the plantation land was sold and the house left to deteriorate.

A century after construction of the plantation's big house, George

B. Crozat, a New Orleans dentist, restored it, furnishing it with outstanding pieces of Louisiana furniture. With his architect, Douglas Freret, Crozat fashioned a landscape that would complement the magnificent mansion. Since the ancient live oaks between the house and the river shaded most of the front garden, Crozat decided on a garden with parterre allusions behind the house. The garden at the Governor's Palace at Colonial Williamsburg, then newly designed and installed, seems to have impressed him. The landscape architect at the Governor's Palace was Arthur Shurcliff, who restored and designed so many of the gardens of colonial plantation houses in Virginia that his name cannot be severed from the garden movement of the 1930s and 1940s now called Colonial Revival.

Houmas House is connected to the original four-room dwelling behind it, and is flanked by unusual two-story hexagonal *garconnières,* quarters for the young men of the family. To the right of the house, there is still a cistern.

Houmas House is a monument to the foresight of Crozat, one of a small group of Louisianians who in the first half of the twentieth century recognized the significance and vulnerability of the state's architectural and garden heritage and expended great effort in stabilizing irreplaceable cultural resources.

Wisteria arch

Urns and ivy

Garçonnière

Stairs of *garçonnière*

Audubon State Commemorative Area and
Oakley Plantation
Near St. Francisville

It is scarcely possible to think of Oakley plantation without also thinking of John James Audubon, the naturalist and illustrator who in 1821 arrived in West Feliciana Parish to teach drawing to Eliza Pirrie, the daughter of Oakley's owners. During Audubon's four-month stint at Oakley, he painted thirty-two of his birds of America. The comments he set down about the region are invaluable because of his alertness regarding flora and fauna. In his journal he described the "rich magnolias covered with fragrant blossoms" that he encountered in Oakley's neighborhood, as well as the beeches, poplars, and hollies, and the "numberless warblers and thrushes."

Still, Oakley has much more to its story than its intersection with the life of Audubon. The house, built about 1806, makes a very straightforward response to the local climate and building materials, without the austerity and self-consciousness of later plantation houses in the parish. The kitchen behind the house is not original but was reconstructed on the foundations of the original and affords a sense both of the scale of the outbuilding it replaces and of the intimate and constant connection between the big house and the kitchen.

Ornamental gardens were probably near the house. The parterre to the left of the house was a gift of a garden club in New Orleans and is strictly conjectural. It is, however, an excellent instance of the kind of Colonial Revival boxwood parterre that appeared on the eastern seaboard in the 1930s and 1940s, particularly where the Garden Club of Virginia laid out gardens for plantation houses along the James River. Today this small garden room at Oakley is nearly sixty years old, and historic in its own right.

The nearby cold frame is evidence of the self-sufficiency of the plantation gardeners. It was used to grow ornamentals and kitchen plants from seeds and cuttings and to propagate and protect them during the colder months.

The naturalistic pathways in the commemorative area contrast vestiges of the indigenous forest against more recent additions to the ground cover.

Today Oakley is owned and operated by the Louisiana Office of State Parks.

House and cold frame

Sculpture, rear view

Cast iron garden seat

Sundial garden and oak branches

Slave cabins

Statue in the woods

Rosedown
St. Francisville

The twenty-eight-acre gardens of Rosedown are singular among Louisiana's plantation landscapes in the amount of information recorded about them and the condition of the surviving fabric. Built in the 1830s by Daniel and Martha Turnbull, Rosedown was purchased in 1956 by the Catherine Fondren Underwood family, of Houston. The Underwoods painstakingly restored the house and gardens and opened them to the public. They cleared and tended the grounds under the guidance of Ralph Gunn, a landscape architect from Houston. The stewardship the Underwoods exercised over forty years ensured not only the survival but the prosperity of the plantation. Today Rosedown is one of the most frequently visited gardens in Louisiana.

The maker of Rosedown's gardens was Martha Hilliard Barrow Turnbull, the mistress of the plantation from the 1830s until she died, in 1896. As a young married couple, she and her husband visited the great gardens of the Continent on their grand tour. She imported the Carrara marble sculptures that line the allée, and she carried home images of formality and axiality, as well as a heightened interest in anything horticultural. As she developed an orchard, kitchen garden, and pleasure garden, she also built a horticultural infrastructure: a cold pit, a large conservatory near the house, and a gardener's shed. What is especially valuable, she kept a methodical record of her daily work in the gardens.

Like most plantation mistresses, Turnbull had to assume weighty responsibilities when her husband was away on business, as a planter often was. She not only had to look after the gardens but had to take charge of clothing, feeding, and managing the health of a substantial slave population. Her diary leaves no doubt that the daily life of a woman on the plantation was more than hoopskirts and leisure. Days and years of hard work and worry show through her words. The greater number of her notations have to do with the kitchen garden as she labored to produce fruit and vegetables sufficient for her family. She also propagated ornamentals seasonally.

Among the vegetables she planted were asparagus, beets, cabbage, carrots, celery, eggplants, mustard, parsnips, potatoes, princess English peas, radishes, salsify, spring lettuce, tomatoes, and turnips. She often remarked on the difficulty she had in establishing an orchard. Among the flowers she grew from seed were coreopsis, dahlias, hollyhocks, pinks, snapdragons, and sweet williams. By cuttings she multiplied her camellias, boxwood, and roses. She described a hedge of wild peach and roses. In November, 1844, she mentioned that she had set out layers from shrubs in the "children's garden"—possibly an area set aside so her children might practice gardening. Often she wrote of her work in the greenhouse and of putting out the greenhouse plants in May. In January, 1849, she made the entry, "Let out the Orangery today." In December, 1855, she noted that she had repaired "every pain of glass in both hot-beds." Only one of those hotbeds survives today.

On March 1, 1850, she proclaimed, "My garden in perfect order. All my spring Vegetables up. The large flag Leek that Mr. Ryan sewed in May are first rate." Interspersed are notes on formulas and recipes for fertilizers. In 1850, she recommended that "For Moss Roses in December put to a Bushel of Woodsearth a Bushel of manure one Pint of Lime to be worked around the bushes."

In 1853, she conducted an inventory at her orchard by the creek: "many peach trees, 8 blue figs, 2 pear trees, 11 apples, 9 quince, 30 azaleas, 13 heliotrope, 15 red flowers from coast." The list suggests that her orchard was not strictly an orchard and that she was using that piece of rich earth to grow some of her ornamental cuttings. In November of the same year she commented that some of her camellias—in her word, Japonicas—had taken root, but she went on in the same entry to remark that she had bought twenty-four. She was apparently impatient with her low rate of success. Then the following May she noted, "We had 50 Japonicas to come up from the seed—it is good to keep the ground around them covered with leaves to keep in the moisture."

Her projects year after year lead us to believe that she was truly an experimental gardener, never satisfied with the status quo and always eager to test a new idea. On November 20, 1855, she exulted, "The roses are beautiful. We have taken up all the shrubs on one side, and filled the Loomhouse lot, and now spading and putting in complete order before they go on the other side. My orange trees are full of Oranges." But like all gardeners, she also had experimental failures: "My cauliflower will not do at all. The bloom size of a dime." Her gardens were the lenses through which she viewed the world. And when the Civil War came, her garden and her world came crashing in around her. Her husband died shortly after the war began, and she spent the remainder of her life at Rosedown as a widow. She wrote on February 10, 1869, "I feel perfectly discouraged. Not one thing towards making a garden done. Garden looks deplorable. I see no seed coming up [because of] the repeated and heavy rains since Christmas." But she continued to plant flowers as well as vegetables, although she began to refer frequently to her truck patch and the prices she was able to get. The story that emerges from the pages of Turnbull's diary is that of a woman who found in the act of gardening eternal hope, even in the face of the hardest adversity. In 1893, she was eighty-four. Yet her entries scarcely manifest how much had changed since she began shaping Rosedown as a young bride: "Washed my windows. Put out Tuberoses & White La France & Papa Guntier roses. . . . Nearly every walk on both sides clean and nice. Quite advanced in Garden work. . . . Put down layers of Frenchmans. Variegated Red & White Japonicas. Beautiful spring day."

Oak allée

Figures of South America and North America

North America

Sculpture against conservatory wall

Urn

Urn in pool

Fountains and summerhouse

Butler Greenwood, or Lower Greenwood Bains

Butler Greenwood was established as a plantation on approximately 2200 acres obtained in 1786 through a Spanish land grant. The simple main house, built in the early 1800s, was embellished in the 1850s with architectural details that included dormers in the Gothic style. The publications of Andrew Jackson Downing, among them *A Treatise on the Theory and Practice of Landscape Gardening, Adapted to North America,* published in 1841, caused such adornments to be in demand on the East Coast and spread the aesthetic of English romanticism throughout the United States.

Bayou Sara, the watercourse, formed the western boundary of the plantation and enabled a direct water connection to Bayou Sara, the settlement, at its confluence with the Mississippi. As for most early plantations in the area, what made the site practical was its water access. Bayou Sara, the predecessor of St. Francisville and a booming market center, was a link to the ports of Baton Rouge and New Orleans. In 1850, Bayou Sara was the largest port between New Orleans and Memphis and a hub of social interchange. Repeated flooding by the Mississippi, damage by a fire in 1850, and the later competition against water transport by rail lines eventually impelled a relocation of the settlement up the hill at the current site of St. Francisville.

The ornamental landscape at Greenwood was extensive. A magnificent grove of live oaks marks the front of the property, achieving a deep separation from the road. The house stands on a central spine of high ground, from which the land drops away dramatically on both sides as a result of the easily eroded loess on the eastern side of the river from Baton Rouge to Natchez. The areas flanking the high ground became sunken or terraced gardens. An ancient female ginkgo tree now shades the north garden, and an intricate wooden summerhouse survives as the centerpiece of what was once a boxwood parterre. Only a few of the boxwood plants have survived. The layout of the garden was measured and recorded between 1935 and 1941 as part of the Historic American Buildings Survey. Lower Greenwood was the only garden in Louisiana recorded during the original phase of HABS. The only other gardens included in that phase were in Massachusetts.

On the upper terrace of the right-hand garden an extension of the boxwood parterre centers on a sundial ringed by upside-down ceramic ale bottles half-buried in the ground. The beds enclosed by the boxwood contain remnants of spirea, azalea, sweet olive, magnolia fuscata, and camellia. Behind the parterre stands the concrete outline of the cold frame, probably in service from the early 1920s until approximately 1940, the years that a mail-order nursery, Feliciana Gardens, operated at Greenwood.

The collection of iron garden ornaments and furnishings on display in front of the house is exceptional in its range and detail. Urns on pedestals add an air of formality to the feel of the grove of live oaks. The side gardens rely on standard conventions of eighteenth- and nineteenth-century garden design—the geometric parterre and the evergreen palette—but the grid of live oaks is unique in being neither formal nor informal. The trees are planted in almost geometric order. It is as if the designer wavered between the two poles of garden style and reached a compromise.

The commercial operation of Feliciana Gardens meant expansion for the gardens. The nursery ledger reveals that most of the plants sold were azaleas and camellias but that the bulbs of spider lilies, daffodils, rain lilies, and red lycoris were also popular.

Today a seventh-generation descendant of the original settlers lives at Greenwood, carefully looking after this rare vestige of a significant nineteenth-century garden.

The gardens of Lower Greenwood were once almost as elaborate as those of nearby Rosedown, but time has taken its toll, particularly in the decline and death of some of the plants. The visitor, however, has the rare privilege of viewing a nineteenth-century landscape that has not undergone extensive restoration or had new layers added to it. What survives testifies to a past with an extremely interesting spatial composition, a rich planting scheme, and an outstanding collection of garden ornaments.

Live oak trunk and shed

Tree roots

Camellias and boxwood

Summerhouse in sunken garden

Sundial and bottle ring

Cast iron garden bench

Stairway to well garden

Well

Stairway from well garden

Afton Villa
St. Francisville

Afton Villa has worn many faces and passed through many incarnations. One of the cluster of notable garden landscapes in West Feliciana Parish, the estate survives today only in its magnificent gardens. In 1849, the planter David Barrow and his second wife, Susan, built the house, a rare instance of Gothicism in the area, around the frame of an earlier house. The romantic naturalism of Downing influenced the architecture and the garden design. Much like Lower Greenwood, Afton Villa was in a parklike setting, with only the gardens immediately adjacent to the dwelling formal and geometric. Susan, who was from Kentucky, had traveled widely on the eastern seaboard. Well read, she was probably aware of the vogue of Gothic romanticism. She wanted her house to be in style, and a picturesque villa with Gothic Revival details answered that desire. The name Afton is said to come from a poem by Robert Burns that was a favorite of David's daughter Mary. The Barrows followed Downing's model so faithfully that they made the kitchen part of the house itself rather than a detached building. Fire destroyed the house in 1963, leaving just the gardens and a pile of rubble to tell of former grandeur.

Unlike many plantations, Afton Villa has had a succession of unrelated owners since its builders died. The ten owners have left an imprint on the land by their diverse uses of it and the designs they have introduced. Nevertheless, the original configuration is not wholly lost.

We owe to the landscape architect Theodore Landry much of what we know about the earlier landscape at Afton Villa. Landry and his wife were always meticulous about listing what they found on a historic site before beginning renovations. When he worked at Afton Villa for Dorothy Nobel Percy in 1952, he first did a plane table survey of the site as it was. He discovered the scant remains of a rose garden, a maze, and a geometric parterre with three large magnolia fuscatas.

Afton Villa demonstrates how landscape design can make the most of distinctive topographical conditions. The house and half-mile entrance drive were on the highest and most level portions of the site. From that high plateau, the land drops away dramatically in all directions, across the bluffs and ravines that typify the Felicianas. Bayou Sara runs along the western edge of the property; the bottomlands by the stream were planted, mostly in cotton. Barrow's greater agricultural success came from his more fertile holdings across the river, in Pointe Coupee Parish, where he produced sugarcane.

Landry's photographs show the entrance to Afton as a crescent-shaped area with a Gothic-arched carriage gate and carved wooden pedestrian gates. In a spacious parklike area, a winding allée of double rows of live oaks underplanted with azaleas leads to the house. It is not certain how this differs from the original arrangement. Two sculptures and an urn or olive jar, all of indefinite age, are the only garden ornaments in Landry's pictures of the property. The maze garden now holds a statue of a young girl feeding birds from seed in her apron which is believed to be one of the original pieces on the site.

The most elaborate part of the garden scheme was on the south side of the house, where seven terraces—six of which survive today—led down in the direction of Bayou Sara to the steep ravine. Many changes have occurred on this side of the house as a result of erosion, neglect, and overgrowth, and because the terraces have been put to growing crops. We will probably never know how things started out. The uppermost terrace has a low masonry retaining wall at its edge, with a central flight of stairs connecting the next terrace. Eight sets of stairs still remain. Several sources describe greenhouses at the foot of the terraces, near the drop-off to the ravine.

The 1850 census recorded eighteen slave houses but not where they were placed. A family cemetery is prominently situated to the left of the house, near the front, and a high evergreen hedge encloses it.

Landry kept the formal parterre elements of the upper terrace where they were and based the rest of his plan as much as possible on the locations of persistent flowering bulbs. The symmetrical butterfly beds at the center are believed original; Landry positioned a sundial in the center of this garden, on the spot of an earlier iron gazebo. The layout of the original maze was not clear, and the current maze is Landry's own design. In his final plan for the gardens, Landry eliminated the rose garden, replacing it with a linear boxwood maze. That decision may have been based on the client's wish for simplified maintenance.

In 1972, Morrell and Genevieve Trimble, of New Orleans, purchased Afton Villa and began more than twenty years of arduous and loving care and improvement of the property. Today the visitor sees the rewards of their labor, much of it done with the advice of the landscape architect Neil Odenwald. They added a pond southeast of the house below the terrace level, and nature walks through the Valley Garden connect the lowest terrace to the pond. The walks and the banks of the pond have been planted with thousands of naturalizing bulbs, primarily daffodils.

Building Afton Villa around an older house was a romantic and sentimental gesture. The Trimbles' decision to create a ruins garden among the remains of the house's foundations similarly shares in the romantic aesthetic that informed the site's original character. The basement and perimeter foundation walls are barely visible beneath the cover of seasonal blooms and ground covers. The basement floor is now a patio where visitors can rest and where there is space for receptions and entertainment.

Ruins Garden

Tulips and Ruins Garden

Spring bloom

Sculpture and wisteria

Peacock on terrace

Azaleas and wisteria

Parterre and pansies

The Garden of Valcour Aime: Le Petit Versailles Near Vacherie

There was a miniature river, meandering in and out and around the beautifully kept parterres, the tiny banks of which were an unbroken mass of blooming violets. . . . There were summer houses draped with strange, foreign-looking vines; a pagoda on a mound, the entrance of which was reached by a flight of steps. It was an octagonal building, with stained-glass windows. . . . Further on was—a mountain! covered from base to top with beds of blooming violets. A narrow, winding path led to the summit, from which a comprehensive view was obtained of the extensive grounds, bounded by a series of conservatories.

—Eliza Ripley, *Social Life in Old New Orleans, Being Recollections of My Girlhood* (1912)

When Eliza Ripley visited Valcour Aime's plantation in March, 1847, the gardens, begun in 1842, had all the hallmarks of a *jardin anglais,* then in fashion in France. What appeared strange and exotic to most Louisianians would have fitted in with the finest estates of the French countryside. In 1836, Aime had bought the property in St. James Parish from his brother-in-law, Jacques Telesphore Roman, who eventually built a house, Bon Séjour—today Oak Alley—on an adjacent tract that Aime sold him. Aime remodeled Roman's French colonial house but retained its Creole one-room-deep floor plan. He added wings to the back and dressed the exterior with Greek Revival details. For his pleasure grounds, he looked to France for direction. Who designed Aime's gardens remains cloudy, since the evidence is that Joseph Muller, who trained at the Jardin des Plantes, in Paris, and whom some suppose responsible, arrived at the plantation in 1852, when the gardens had already been completed.

Aime's garden was organized around a rivulet, or La Rivière, and a basin in front of the house. The water features were excavated, and water pumped from the Mississippi filled them. On September 3, 1842, Aime first mentioned the garden's construction in his diary: "Prepared the ground for an 'English Park' and dug a basin in front of the dwelling house with over one hundred and twenty hands." Thereafter references occur in the diary to the work of building the garden and to specific plants in it, but they are scattered among Aime's notations about his sugar operation. Aime was one of the most successful sugar planters in the state and adopted innovative and progressive refining techniques. He traveled to Cuba to study the technology there, and on his travels to tropical regions, he collected exotics, which he protected in his hothouses. In 1843, he described using eighty cords of wood "to heat hothouses" on a particularly cold February night. In March, 1843, the garden was still under construction, and Aime recorded "hauling river sand with six carts for the alleys of the park." By October, 1844, the rivulet and paths were in place and the ground was being prepared for planting. During that month he wrote, "Hauled to English Park 1500 loads of manure in one month, with two carts; with four carts and four loaders, hauled to English Park one thousand loads of dirt in seven days." In April, 1845, Aime commented that he was finished hauling sand and dirt to the garden.

The garden was punctuated by pavilions and ornamental features. Unlike the neoclassical summerhouses that no doubt stood on other plantations of the period, all the structures Aime built were either rustic or exotic and contributed to the picturesque quality that was the *jardin anglais'* objective. Ripley's memory of a Chinese pagoda is not corroborated independently, but such a structure would have been a stock feature in this sort of garden in France and the foundation of an octagonal structure has been discovered atop the mound. The mound itself was intended as camouflage and insulation for a domed, grottolike icehouse, which survives in the ruined garden. On the edge of the rivulet was a miniature fortress, named La Roche de Ste. Hélène, after the island on which Napoleon spent his exile. It was a favorite playground for Aime's five children and numerous grandchildren. Near the basin was a cascade constructed of faux rockwork; the story has been passed along of an iron swan that sat on the rock formation squirting water down the cascade.

Each of the several bridges across the rivulet was unique. The archives at Tulane hold a photograph of a Chinese bridge that is no longer there. Theodore Landry and his wife measured and drew a masonry bridge with parapet sidewalls in the 1940s; today only the brick arched span exists. Aime mentioned the bridge's construction in 1853: "Finished on the 10th the stone bridge. There was still 4 days work to lay on the stones on the sides and underneath. This will be done on Sundays." It appears that after Aime's initial garden scheme was fully executed and flourishing, he continued to add structures.

The Landrys also drew a plane table survey of the garden in the 1940s, and this is the only scale drawing that exists of the garden. Of course, by 1940 the garden was completely different from what it had been. An open, sunny garden with wooded edges had become a forestlike mass. In the park's original design, an open green lawn lay in the center of the rivulet's loop. In September, 1849, Aime wrote that "the batture and the road in front of the garden are entirely overflowed; the center lawn is under water." A month later, he again remarked that "the water has overflowed the center lawn."

In 1846, Gabriel, Aime's youngest child and only son, left New Orleans for a grand tour, one of two extended trips to the Continent that the young man was to take. In Europe, Gabriel visited landmarks, went to the opera, and searched out persons experienced in manufacturing who might work for his father. In January, 1847, Gabriel set down his impressions of Versailles in his diary:

> I went to Versailles with Mr. de Crozant. It corresponds with my preconceived ideas of what the ancient residence of the great Louis XIV should be. I did not expect anything less of the magnificence and pride of the monarch who stamped his name on the century which glories on more than one score in having witnessed his birth. Those ponds, those bastions, those stairways, those groves, those fountains, and that prodigious work done by the arms of workmen makes one dream of the superb Babylon. Heaven grant that the people respect those monuments of a king destined to be forever illustrious.

Little did Gabriel realize how prophetic his words were. Certainly he could not have imagined that his father would one day be called the Louis XIV of Louisiana, and his plantation Le Petit Versailles.

At French palaces, Gabriel would have seen not only the axial geometry of the seventeenth century but also the smaller gardens that exhibited the French version of romantic English naturalism. The *jardin anglo-chinois,* with curving paths, miniature hills and islands, rustic bridges, and pavilions in the Chinese mode, was what they had become. In Italy, Gabriel visited the Boboli Gardens, the Villa Borghese, and other rural villas. The young man's travels were not calculated to yield ideas for his father's garden, which was already complete. Instead, they exposed the Aime heir to the best that Europe had to offer, allowed him to develop a sense of taste and refinement, and perhaps let him look for a suitable bride. A match was never made, however, for when Gabriel disembarked from his second tour, on September 15, 1854, he spent the night in New Orleans. Yellow fever raged in the city, and two days later Gabriel was dead. Valcour Aime's spirit was broken. Two years after that, his wife died, and in 1858 one of his daughters. Aime's work in his garden halted, and soon the Civil War put an end to all normal life on the plantation. On New Year's Day, 1867, Aime died of pneumonia. Fire consumed his house in 1920, and today a recently built one-story dwelling sits in its place, beneath the majestic canopy of the live oaks. Between this house and River Road floats the forest canopy beneath which the rivulet still runs, though a bit sluggishly, and the fortress and mound still provide a prospect over the surrounding fields of sugarcane.

Rivulet

La Roche de Ste. Hélène

Bridge

Cascade rockwork

Cascade

Miniature fortress and rivulet

Rivulet and magnolia trunk

Into the Twentieth Century:
Revivalism and the Age of Estate Gardens

*The evident harmony of arrangement between house and the surrounding
landscape is what strikes one in Italian landscape architecture—the design
as a whole including gardens, terraces, groves, and their necessary surroundings and embellishments, it being clear that no one of these component parts
was ever considered independently.*

—Charles Platt, *Italian Gardens* (1894)

Shadows-on-the-Teche
New Iberia

The story of the landscape at Shadows-on-the-Teche is that of four generations of one family—of the layers of imprints that David and Mary Clara Weeks and their descendants left on their property along the banks of Bayou Teche. Originally two hundred acres in the tiny settlement of New Iberia, the grounds are today a scant two acres near the center of the bustling town of New Iberia. In some ways, though, things have changed only slightly. The town and the region still mark the seasons by the cycle of sugarcane farming, and the cultivation and refining of sugar is still a major component of the economy and the culture. David Weeks built the Shadows so that his family would be nearer to society. His large holdings were on nearby Grand Cote (now Weeks Island), one of the amazing salt domes of this marshy area near Louisiana's Gulf Coast.

David Weeks began constructing the house at the Shadows in the early 1830s, but it is the landscape design that William Weeks Hall, the last in the Weeks family to own the place, inaugurated in 1922 that prevails there today.

Hall's garden was not without reference to and respect for its predecessors. Originally, the house, on the crest of the natural levee, had a planted yard at the front, on the side toward the main road. The back, toward the bayou, faced the work yard, with its slave dwellings, outside kitchen, and other outbuildings. The kitchen garden, often referred to in the family papers, may have been on the town side, immediately across the road from the front garden. Adrien Persac painted two views of the house in 1861, and these paintings, one of the front and the other of the back, are the only pictures we have predating photographs of the building. There is a family photograph that was taken in front of the house about 1870. The correspondence between Mary Clara and her adult children attests that the care of the ornamental and kitchen gardens was of great interest to her. Her love of gardening was shared particularly by her daughter Harriet (Allie) and her son and daughter-in-law, William and Mary Conrad Weeks. From the more than seventeen thousand family documents surviving, especially the letters and receipts, it is possible to piece together a sense of daily life. There are few letters by Mary Clara, but those she wrote to her second husband, John Moore, when he was serving in the United States Congress, express her sensibilities and her attachment to her garden. On March 4, 1852, she related, "After a severe winter Spring has to all appearances set in. The flowers that disappeared ever since the snow have again begun to bloom, the china and other trees to put out, the peach trees are full of bloom. I am very busy in the garden, have planted many things in the new Garden. I had green peas on the table every day when the freeze came in January." On November 28, she acknowledged, "In dark bad weather when I cannot go in the Garden time hangs heavy on my hands. . . . You cannot think how industrious I have got. Every day I am out all the time. The Gardens are all full of trash and many things to move." On January 14, 1853, she continued in the same vein: "You know the monotony of Attakapas life, only varied by the fear of freezes or of sickness. . . . I am now busy removeing and trimming shrubbery, and cleaning off litter preparatary to sewing Seed. George is interested and works well at the shrubbery." Mary Clara often requested that her husband send her seeds of flowering plants from Washington. She also ordered roses, fruit trees, and "pyramidal cypresses" from Thomas Affleck, the nurseryman and popular journalist who wrote on horticulture in *De Bow's Review* and in his own almanac. Ornamental plants were much in demand during the time, and one letter describes a plant salesman peddling his wares from a flatboat on Bayou Teche.

In 1861, at the onset of the Civil War, the Weeks family was prospering and had accomplished much toward improving the grounds at the Shadows. But that changed very quickly. Moore refused to sign the loyalty oath to the Union, and the family dispersed through north Louisiana and Texas to wait out the war. Mary Clara remained at the Shadows, but while separated from her husband and children, she fell ill. In 1863, the Union army came to New Iberia, and the commander set up headquarters in her house. He occupied the bottom floor, and Mary Clara stayed upstairs. Too weak to travel, she died in her bed. She was buried in the garden west of the house, because a cemetery burial was difficult under Union occupation.

After the war and then the death of Moore, William Weeks, the eldest son, and his family moved into the Shadows and made an effort to rebuild the fences and remedy the wear and tear of the occupation and neglect. They added plants and stayed true to his mother's devotion to ornamental horticulture. Their daughter, Lily Weeks, who was particularly fond of gardening, grew up caring for the garden. She married Gilbert Hall, a lawyer originally from New York who was living in New Orleans, after a ten-year courtship. The couple had in common a love of beautiful scenery and reading, above all romantic novels, as well as a fondness of flowers. But the family resided in New Orleans so that Hall could retain his law practice,

leaving the Shadows with only a caretaker. The grounds suffered, and the outbuildings fell into disrepair.

When Hall's health failed, the family moved to Kansas City, where he had relatives. He died in 1909, and Lily and their young son, William Weeks Hall, moved back to New Orleans. With little means, Lily managed in 1913, to send the young man to study at the Pennsylvania Academy of the Fine Arts, where he won a traveling scholarship to Europe. The friendships he forged with fellow artists at the school, along with the experiences of his European tour, were to affect deeply Hall's outlook and actions as an artist. In France, he observed Claude Monet painting his water lilies in the gardens at Giverny and viewed the cubist works of Pablo Picasso and the abstractions of Henri Matisse. He developed a keen eye in art and design, and a particular responsiveness to light and color. Hall's approach in designing the gardens at the Shadows was to celebrate luminosity and color much as the impressionists did.

In 1919, preparing to set out on his European tour, he reached the decision that, once his travels were over, he would return to his homeplace in New Iberia and undertake the preservation of the house and the revitalization of its landscape. He hired an architect, Richard Koch, from New Orleans, for the restoration. Hall razed the brick outbuildings that were beyond saving and eventually paved a terrace and garden walks with the old bricks. He planned a rectangular garden room centering on a clump of camellias planted in the nineteenth century, added garden sculpture and furniture, and installed a shallow fishpond where a greenhouse once stood. He visited plantations of the region to acquire a sense of the kind of design appropriate for the house. Hall's intention from the outset was to restore and maintain the Shadows as his home during his lifetime and then to leave the property to a public trust so that the public might enjoy it for generations to come. Arranging this proved more difficult than Hall had ever foreseen, but finally, in 1958, as he lay dying in the hospital, the National Trust for Historic Preservation wired him that they accepted the terms of his bequest. He died the next day.

Hall's life at the Shadows was the stuff of legends. He was influential as a painter and was a member of the New Orleans Arts and Crafts Club, where he associated with a community of artists that made an impact on the history of the arts in the region—artists like Caroline Durieux, Enrique Alferez, A. Boyd Cruise, and William Woodward. In later life, Hall turned reclusive and rarely left the Shadows, but he maintained a lively correspondence with writers, filmmakers, plantsmen, and gardeners across the country. During the 1930s and 1940s many a novelist and filmmaker made a pilgrimage to the Shadows to meet this unusual man and see the place around which such a mystique had grown up. Henry Miller immortalized Hall's Shadows in *The Air-Conditioned Nightmare,* published in 1945: "I could hear Weeks Hall's booming voice saying to me: 'I should like to do a garden which would not be a seed-catalogue by daylight, but strange, sculptural blossoms by night, things hanging in trees and moving like metronomes, transparent plastics in geometrical shapes, silhouettes lit by light and changing with the changing hours. A garden is a show—why not make one enormous garden, one big changing show?' " Hall expressed definite ideas about garden design and planting. In a letter to a friend in New Orleans, he broached concepts that would not become mainstream before the 1980s:

> As I said, a garden to me means form and color. The cultural side is routine and entirely experiment unless common things are grown in good combinations. I do not look through seed catalogs half as much as I watch for roadside gardens which have lusty things which I can adapt to my uses. Sometimes they work, sometimes not. But, they must function as color which gratifies the eye.
>
> I merely suggest some combinations which are pretty swell and very simply done. Exposure and soil will have to be tried, but once established these ordinary things should be very beautiful. . . . Visualize the broad effects, and use them where and if you can.

Hall became an accomplished plantsman himself and an expert on camellias. He communicated with growers in the Mobile area and was a frequent customer and correspondent of Edward Avery McIlhenny, who ran a nursery on Avery Island.

Hall prepared two notebooks as a guide to the history, maintenance, and care of the Shadows. About his custody of his home-place, he wrote, "I have never considered myself anything but a trustee of something fine which chance has put in my hands to preserve. Fine things are without value, in that they belong only to those rare people who appreciate them beyond any price. It is to those people that I should like to entrust the place."

Sculpture and aspidistra

Sculpture of Winter

Fishpond and water lilies

Second sculpture of Winter

Olive jar

Wisteria

Oak and yucca

Hattendorf oak trunk

Rice-paper plants and Bayou Teche

Longue Vue Gardens
7 Bamboo Road
New Orleans

Edith and Edgar Stern left a considerable legacy to the city of New Orleans through their philanthropy, but nothing as enduring as Longue Vue, the house and gardens that they donated to the public. Stern was a cotton broker and his wife an heiress to a Sears, Roebuck fortune. Both were well traveled and admirers of the arts and fine things. Edith Stern, who was especially fond of William Weeks Hall, wrote him in 1934 to try to persuade him to receive Ellen Biddle Shipman, an East Coast garden designer who was lecturing in New Orleans and whom she had urged to visit Shadows-on-the-Teche during her sojourn in Louisiana: "The landscape gardener Ellen Shipman is about to descend on you. We have just presented her as a lecturer at heavy loss. 'We' is our genteel garden club and the Arts and Crafts Club." By this time, Hall was extraordinarily retiring and altogether averse to socializing. When Shipman turned up on his doorstep, he pretended not to be at home, but she toured the gardens anyway. She wrote to thank him: "Your wonderful place and the hours we spent there is so impressed upon my mind that I shall never forget it. I honestly know of no other small piece of property so beautifully and admirably treated—it holds within its corpus every element that the pleasure grounds surrounding a home should have. It has a lesson within its gates that

I wish all people could learn, at least all landscape architects. . . . For your Forebears part, I give thanks; for your part, I honor you." Although Edith Stern was not impressed with Shipman's lectures, she was extremely enthusiastic about her design work. When the Sterns decided to develop a garden on Bamboo Road at their residence, Shipman gained the commission. In 1935, she began the project, traveling to Louisiana frequently. At Shipman's prompting, the Sterns concluded that they needed to build a new house to complement the monumental simplicity of the proposed garden and to take better advantage of the site. On Shipman's advice, they hired the New York architectural firm of William and Geoffrey Platt, with whom Shipman had often collaborated.

Shipman's landscape scheme had as its highlight a long rectangular garden room bisected by an axis that led the eye from the south portico of the new house to a reflecting pool and circular temple. Tree-form camellias lined the space. Beyond the formal garden was a large kitchen garden combining vegetables, fruits, and flowers, and greenhouses and cold frames. And beyond that was the "wild garden" installed in 1940 for plants indigenous to the Gulf South, particularly a collection of Louisiana iris. Still farther on was a two-story brick *pigeonnier* modeled after the one at Uncle Sam plantation, near Convent. Shipman also reworked the frontal view of the house by creating a live oak allée to enframe it.

In 1966, after her husband's death, Edith Stern traveled to Spain with William Platt. Inspired by the long, narrow water channels of Spanish gardens like the Alhambra and the Generalife, she and Platt reworked Shipman's south garden room by adding an axis of water down the middle of the broad rectangular lawn panel. The Pan Garden and the Yellow Garden, small courtyardlike garden rooms, are adjacent to the house. Dotting the gardens are sculptural pieces, some traditional and some starkly modern. The contrast of these bespeaks the Sterns' eclectic tastes and their broad appreciation for the traditional as well as the avant-garde.

Longue Vue Gardens opened to the public in 1968, and the house opened as a museum of decorative arts in 1980. Both house and garden nod to the antebellum traditions of Louisiana. The Greek Revival facade reads like a miniature version of a white-columned plantation house. The allée of live oaks underplanted with ground cover is a smaller version of the traditional oak allée. Its magnificently simple ground plane and the overhead enclosure of the oak canopy make for one of the most effective landscaped spaces anywhere in the South. Camellias, magnolias, and other traditional evergreens are planted throughout.

Entry walk to Spanish Garden

Kumquat in Spanish Garden

Urn, holly fern, and callas

Canal Garden

Sunken fountain

Pigeonnier in Wild Garden

Pool in Wild Garden

Bench and frost-nipped azaleas

Bougainvillea in greenhouse area

Sago palm in Wild Garden

Jungle Gardens
Avery Island

The "island" that the Jungle Gardens are situated on is an eight-mile-high and six-mile-wide mountain of salt, the top of which protrudes above the surrounding marshes. It appears an island since the waters of Bayou Petite Anse surround it. Five such geologic formations are along the Gulf Coast. The salt mines near the coast of Louisiana are among the largest in the world and are 1100 feet below the surface of the islands.

The family that settled at Avery Island in 1818 has earned several fortunes from the natural resources of the land—first from salt, then from Tabasco peppers, and finally from oil. Salt was discovered on the island in 1790, and John Marsh, of New Jersey, holder of the Spanish land grant to the property, built the first plant for salt extraction during the War of 1812. The plant was of vital importance during the Civil War, because of the desperate need for salt to preserve food for the troops. Marsh's son-in-law, Judge Daniel D. Avery, deepened the mine to meet the demand and donated salt to the Confederacy. Because of the value of the resource, the Union troops forced the Avery and McIlhenny families from the island, flooded the salt mine, and destroyed the sugar plantation and its gardens.

Upon returning to the island, the McIlhennys, according to fam-

ily accounts, found that the only plant to survive in the kitchen garden was the persistent pepper plant that Edmund McIlhenny had grown from seed brought from Mexico. He mashed the peppers with salt and vinegar and invented the sauce that is now a household word. Its name derives from the place in Mexico—Tabasco—from which the pepper seeds came. The Indian word means "land where the soil is humid."

Despite the huge quantities of salt mined each year, and the operation of oil wells since 1942, the island's marshlands are a protected habitat for animals and plants. Although it was Tabasco sauce that first brought Avery Island international exposure, the Jungle Gardens there are perhaps as exotic and fascinating as the unique flavor of the sauce.

It was Edward Avery McIlhenny, born at Avery Island in 1872, who began developing these gardens and who nurtured them over a span of fifty years. Ned McIlhenny spent his youth exploring the woods and marshes of the island, marveling at their biotic diversity. In 1893, after graduating from college, he joined Robert E. Peary's expedition to study migratory birds in the Arctic. The avid naturalist returned home to find that much of the wildlife he had known as a boy had disappeared. He was especially distressed over the loss of egrets and herons resulting from milliners' insatiable demand for their feathers.

McIlhenny became one of the earliest active conservationists in the United States. Because of the work he began in 1892 to save the snowy egret, today more than a hundred thousand egrets return each year to the island's Bird City.

McIlhenny brought home exotics from the many continents he visited in his travels as a naturalist. He founded the McIlhenny nursery, an extensive wholesale and retail grower and landscape-contracting business. He supplied camellias, azaleas, bamboos, and other stock plants to the most elaborate gardens along the Gulf Coast. The firm designed and installed the gardens surrounding the new state capitol. McIlhenny was one of the true statesmen of the nursery and horticulture business during the twenties and thirties. He corresponded with collectors of plants and gardeners across the region, advising his customers about proper care and maintenance.

Today the gardens at Avery Island comprise 250 acres, bringing together exotic plants from all over the world. Thirty thousand azaleas, seventeen thousand varieties of irises, four hundred Asian and European varieties of camellias, sixty-five kinds of bamboo, and numerous exotic palms combine into a textural study unequaled anywhere else. There is a Chinese garden on the grounds, with a pagoda and a giant statue of the Buddha. Surrounding the Jungle Gardens is a broad band that the family has reserved as wildlife habitat.

Avery Island must be experienced as the collage of industry, agriculture, horticulture, and nature that makes it the unique and powerful place it is. It is almost sensory overload to drive by the acres of pepper fields full of red fruit and then to see the thousands of white egrets perched above the marsh waters, the stands of bamboo, and the alligators gazing lazily from the slimy green waters. The Jungle Gardens are the centerpiece of this landscape and witness to the zeal and imagination of a family caring for the same land for over a century and a half.

Tree trunk, road, and marsh

Basin in camellia garden

Winter trees and marsh grasses

Azalea

Fallen azalea petals

Azaleas and clearing with oaks

Azaleas

Path through bamboo

Golden bamboo

Buddha's lagoon from Moon Bridge

Moon Bridge

Holly Road

Windrush Gardens
Rural Life Museum, Baton Rouge

In 1921, the twenty-one-year-old Steele Burden began designing and building a collection of formal gardens adjacent to his family home, Windrush plantation. His family had moved back to the property a few years before, and Burden had spent his early manhood visiting the sites of Louisiana plantations and often working in the maintenance and improvement of plantation grounds, particularly at The Cottage, the Conrad family mansion below Baton Rouge. That magnificent house was destroyed by fire in the 1960s, and there are only scant remains of the once elaborate gardens. Burden became familiar, through his fieldwork, with the typical plant stock of many of these sites: camellias and azaleas under a canopy of live oaks, with luxuriant shade-loving ground covers—aspidistra, liriope, and mondo grass—filling and lining geometric beds. The knowledge he acquired was the foundation of his eventual reputation as a landscape designer sensitive to the character of tropical Louisiana plantation gardens. Windrush Gardens are among hundreds of properties, both historic and new, that Burden invested with a traditional landscape during his long career.

Members of the Burden family have been extraordinarily creative and generous in their philanthropies to enrich the cultural life of Baton Rouge. Burden and his sister Ione lived at Windrush most of their adult lives and created a haven from the metropolitan sprawl that was surrounding the once rural plantation. The family donated 350 acres to Louisiana State University for use as an agricultural and horticultural experiment station. In the 1960s and 1970s, Burden began collecting vestiges of the rural life he saw vanishing from the countryside. He was a thorough and consummate collector, acquiring farm implements, industrial equipment, transportation artifacts, and entire buildings. Eventually his collection grew into the much larger idea of the Rural Life Museum, an outdoor museum for all aspects of life in rural Louisiana.

Burden was also a painter and sculptor. In a small brick studio designed to resemble a plantation slave dwelling, Burden did oil paintings, primarily landscapes, and sculptures that are hand-pinched caricatures based on either biblical or rural themes but always with a twist of irony and a humorous title. The collection of tiny caricatures that is housed in the museum reveals Burden's wry, witty outlook.

Windrush Gardens, between the studio and the family's original homestead, manifests the private and reflective side of Burden as a landscape designer. Burden said that the initial purpose of the gardens was to provide an adequate setting for the garden sculpture he had begun collecting on several journeys to Europe as a young man. What he created are linked garden rooms, intimate in scale and responsive to the size, mood, and character of the sculpture. But once he completed the formal parterrelike rooms, he became interested in stretching their scale and style and began clearing and draining swampland beyond them. He constructed a large pond for drainage and as a setting for native Louisiana irises. Cypresses and other native wetland trees mediate the transition from the quiet, intimate scale of the parterre to the more open and meadowlike contours of the extended landscape.

Burden's genius as a designer is evident everywhere at the Rural Life Museum and Windrush Gardens. Along the winding drive to the complex is his trademark grid of regularly spaced trees enclosing the motorist and framing views of cropland in the distance. Remarkably, Burden has provided a place where two strands in the history of Louisiana—agriculture and horticulture—can continue to be explored, experimented with, and celebrated free of the saccharine nostalgia permeating many antebellum sites and in an atmosphere as progressive and modern as it is responsible to the past.

Buddha in sugar kettle

Woman holding flowers

Cast iron garden bench

Athlete and bench

Sculpture at edge of woods

Fighting stags

Faun

Roman soldier and freeze-burned elephant's ears

Nandina and Roman soldier

Bacchus

Detail of Bacchus

Reflection of maiden in pond

New Orleans Botanical Garden
City Park, New Orleans

As early as 1854, a public park occupied some of the land in New Orleans where City Park now lies. In 1911, the Isaac Delgado Museum of Art—today the New Orleans Museum of Art—opened in the park. A golf course, swimming pool, miniature train, bandstand, and tennis courts came later. During the Great Depression, the Works Progress Administration made funds available for the improvement of public recreation facilities and gave employment to designers and artists affected by the downturn. The landscape architect William Wiedorn was hired to prepare a master plan for the park, the lack of which had long been felt an impediment. The Rose Garden, originally conceived as a retreat for New Orleanians struggling through tough years without gardens of their own, was one part of the scheme. That tiny horticultural gem grew into the New Orleans Botanical Garden, today a resource for education as well as for refreshment. It is also now recognized as having an impressive collection of garden ornaments from the Art Deco movement.

Three artists and designers who were to make many lasting contributions to the city collaborated on the Rose Garden: Wiedorn, the sculptor Enrique Alferez, and the architect Richard Koch. Koch had studied architecture in Paris and then worked for the Historic American Buildings Survey, executing measured drawings of build-

ings in danger of being lost. He learned a deep respect for the proportions and materials of early Louisiana structures. The installations he designed for the Rose Garden—a work shed, potting sheds, tool sheds, and cold frames—are masterly applications of the values he had recognized in his fieldwork. But if Koch's outbuildings revive and glorify tradition, other aspects of the garden are decidedly modern. In the garden's sculptural features—the dolphin fountain, the female figures, the concrete benches, and the iron gate—the Art Deco signature of Alferez is evident. Alferez availed himself of the common materials of the twentieth century: poured concrete, steel, and brick. The garden gently unites old and new techniques and the short-lived abstraction of the American Art Deco.

In 1982, the garden was restored by the Friends of City Park and enclosed by a security fence. In 1992, a master plan for the preservation of the Rose Garden led to extensive plantings that expanded it from simply a rose and display garden to a true botanical garden, concerned with plant communities and the various ecosystems of the region.

The garden is under the canopies of mature live oaks. Several buildings enclose its landscaped garden rooms. On the southern end, adjoining Storyland, the popular children's playground with a restored carrousel, is a conservatory and a working horticultural area with the cold frames, raised beds, and storage structures that Koch designed. On the northern end, opposite the conservatory, is the newly constructed Pavilion of the Two Sisters, an elegant facility housing a library and gift shop, as well as space for lectures and catered events.

Today, City Park spreads over fifteen hundred acres and is the fifth largest urban park in the nation. The seven-acre New Orleans Botanical Garden stands at the heart of this magnificent public space, providing exhibits, programs, and a venue for saluting the city's horticultural and botanical wealth.

Christmas dove and Japanese stone lantern

Oak branches and doves

Oak branch, camellia, and dove

Fountain by Enrique Alferez

Arbor and Carolina jessamine

Art arches

Coleus and ginger lily

Mermaid fountain

At Midcentury: Private Gardens as Public Places

In the South there is bloom for every month in the year. But keeping a garden in bloom for four long seasons is different from keeping one in bloom for three short ones. Succession of bloom depends upon the characteristic plant of each period of the year, in combination with others in bloom at the same time. After winter bulbs and shrubs there are daffodils, then tulips, then the long season of iris. Summer begins with day-lilies, and ends with other members of the amaryllis family. In September, gardens filled with red spider-lilies are as gay as in spring and from October until frost there are chrysanthemums.

—Elizabeth Lawrence, *A Southern Garden* (1942)

Rip Van Winkle Gardens on Jefferson Island Near New Iberia

Jefferson Island, a salt dome like Avery Island, is the home of Rip Van Winkle Gardens, developed on the site of the mansion that the actor Joe Jefferson, famous for his stage portrayal of Washington Irving's Rip Van Winkle, built in 1870. Jefferson had purchased what was then known as Orange Island for a hunting and fishing retreat. In 1917, the J. Lyle Bayless family purchased the property from the Jefferson heirs.

After World War II, J. Lyle Bayless, Jr., began to develop gardens on Jefferson Island. He designed and planted a live oak avenue on the approach to the island. Two severe freezes, in 1962 and 1963, destroyed the subtropical plants in his gardens, including a collection of rare bamboos. Hurricanes in 1964 and 1965 destroyed many live oaks and other plantings. But despite the setbacks, Bayless in 1966 hired Geoffrey Wakefield, an English horticulturist, to create and serve as director of Rip Van Winkle Gardens. Wakefield connected his small gardens with a winding path and added a large number of camellias, as well as a conservatory for rare tropicals and, in the Japanese Garden, a teahouse. Bayless was particularly fond of camellias and hybridized many new varieties. In 1978, he donated the gardens and the Jefferson mansion to the Live Oak Gardens Foundation. In 1996, the historic preservationists Carolyn Doerle and Ron Ray purchased the property.

But the principal force behind the landscape on view today at Rip Van Winkle Gardens was the cave-in of the dome and the subsequent flood that devastated much of Jefferson Island on November 20, 1980. The dramatic changes elicited a new resolve to preserve and enhance the historic and scenic spot. Today the gardens mount outstanding seasonal color displays. A commercial and wholesale nursery specializing in plants of the area operates on the island, serving needs earlier met by the McIlhenny nursery, and even before that, by Mary Palfrey Weeks, on Weeks Island, who sold plants to her neighbors.

Camellia

Live oak trunk and azaleas

Ground cover and Jefferson House

Path through bamboo

Well

Oak trunks

Frozen ginger lilies

Gnarled roots

Path leading to cistern

Dead tree trunk and sasanquas

Stairway to lake

ELsong Garden and Conservatory
Monroe

Joseph Biedenharn's family came to Monroe in 1913 from Vicksburg, where he had become the first person in the nation to bottle commercially the recently formulated fountain drink Coca-Cola. His bottling company flourished, and he took his three sons into the business. The family's fortune made it possible for the only daughter, Emy-Lou, to pursue her love of music and the arts. In the 1930s, she toured the European music capitals—London, Copenhagen, Berlin, and Munich—where she won critical acclaim for her rich contralto voice. She left Europe in 1939, as the effects of Hitler's campaigns spread.

After returning, she asked her father, a widower since 1936, to be allowed to transform the working yard of the house built in 1914 on what had become their estate into garden rooms reminiscent of the elegant gardens she had seen in Europe. Her father commissioned C. C. "Pat" Fleming, a distinguished landscape architect from Houston, to execute a garden in which it would be possible to stage the musical performances that were central to Emy-Lou's life. Work began on the garden in 1947.

Emy-Lou was determined to have her garden ornamented with appropriately elegant sculpture. In New Orleans, she collected what became the signature pieces for each of the garden rooms. Throughout there are symbols of music. The largest of the rooms, the great lawn, culminates in the Wagnerian water fountain on the ballet stage.

Emy-Lou Biedenharn died in 1984. Because she had constantly added new elements and new plants, it was decided to continue improving and developing the garden. In 1987, extensive restoration work began; at the same time, the horticultural selections in the garden were expanded. Added were background music, activated through lasers by strolling visitors, a small garden featuring plants of the Bible, to complement the Bible Museum established in 1971, and a conservatory of contemporary design, replacing the run-down glass structures that Emy-Lou had used for many years.

Water goddess

Water goddess, back view

Garden screen

Staircase and foliage

Tropical foliage

Hydrangea blossoms

Tropical plants in conservatory

Japanese garden

Terrace flowers

Hodges Gardens
Near Many

Between the world wars, wealthy industrialists and landholders throughout the southeastern United States drew on their fortunes and invested in the future by developing extensive gardens that would eventually become tourist attractions. Hodges Gardens were begun in the early 1940s by A. J. Hodges, a pioneer conservationist who undertook a vast reforestation project in west central Louisiana. That part of the state has long depended on its timber resources, and it is fitting that this magnificent garden spot was developed as a "garden in the forest."

A part of Hodges' plan was to develop a 4700-acre experimental arboretum, and in the course of planting it, the workers discovered an abandoned stone quarry. Hodges and his wife, Nona Trigg Hodges, recognized the potential of the unique landform and took advantage of the rock ledges in the design of their scenic gardens.

The principal sixty acres of the gardens are arranged with seventy beds for seasonal color, ranging from a spring display of forty thousand tulips to an array of thousands of fall chrysanthemums.

In 1956, Hodges Gardens was opened to the public, and it is today the nation's largest privately operated horticultural parkland and wildlife refuge. The site is laid out around a 255-acre man-made lake, constructed in 1954, which serves as a water source for fountains, pools, and the gardens' watering system, before the water is recycled back to the lake. The gardens offer possibilities for viewing almost every kind of plant community imaginable. The conservatory and greenhouses are filled with collections of tropicals and exotics, and nearly 75 percent of the seasonal plantings are propagated on site.

St. Francis fountain and camellias

Waterway

Rocks and reflections

Pine woods and ferns

Brigadoon Bridge

Red tulips

Bulb beds

Azaleas and woodland path

Reflections in pond

Tulips and azaleas

Zemurray Gardens
Between Loranger and Folsom

The 150-acre Zemurray Gardens are at the heart of one of the state's richest commercial horticultural production areas, in the sandy soil and piney woods northeast of Hammond. Sam and Sarah Zemurray purchased the property in 1928 and resolved to develop their homeplace and its surrounding landscape so as to reinforce the natural beauty of the terrain and native woodlands. They improved an existing dam and spillway, creating twenty-acre Mirror Lake, with its small island and bridge, which forms the garden's centerpiece. Meandering paths follow the irregular shoreline of the lake, shaded by pines that provide a canopy for wildlife and understory plantings. With the help of the horticulturist Howard Schilling, Sarah Zemurray began planting thousands of azaleas, camellias, and dogwoods, all traditional southern garden species that thrived in the acid soils of the understory. These plantings, along with the bloom of many native trees and shrubs, produce a spring display that is unique in its naturalism. The informality of the woodland paths contrasts with the more architectural regularity of many Louisiana gardens and their arrangements of smaller garden rooms.

Today the Zemurray Gardens are maintained as tribute to the Zemurray family and are open to the public during the season of spring bloom, usually in March and early April.

First glimpse of lake

Road and azaleas in spring

Island

Huntress Diana

Azaleas and lake

Azaleas at lake's edge

The Gardens of the American Rose Center
Shreveport

The Gardens of the American Rose Center are dedicated to the honor of only one plant—America's national flower. The center, the home of the American Rose Society, was created in 1972 through contributions from rose lovers the world over. The rose has had a special place in Louisiana gardens since earliest settlement, but today it is enjoying a renaissance unparalleled in the history of the flower. The gardens, carved from a dense pine forest, are organized to demonstrate the ways roses can be used in the home land- scape. At present there are over twenty thousand rose plants of more than 350 varieties planted in sixty individual gardens. Each year North America's finest rose growers provide the gardens with their new introductions. Theme gardens feature specific kinds of roses, including one in which there are old garden roses grown from historic stock.

The gardens are open from February through the end of October, during the rose's strongest blooming seasons in the region.

Rose display

Roses and pine trees

Thornless roses

Red roses

Rose path

St. Francis

Bronze and stainless steel sculpture of tree rose

Pink roses

Bibliography

Affleck, Thomas. *Southern Rural Almanac, and Plantation and Garden Calendar, for 1860.* Washington, Miss., 1860.

Thomas Affleck Papers. Louisiana and Lower Mississippi Valley Collections (LLMVC), Louisiana State University Libraries.

Baton Rouge City-Parish Planning Commission. *Beauregard Town.* Baton Rouge, 1977.

Brasseaux, Carl A. *A Comparative View of French Louisiana, 1699 to 1762: The Journals of Pierre Le Moyne d'Iberville and Jean-Jacques Blaise d'Abbadie.* Lafayette, La., 1981.

Burgner, Gerald. "Butler Greenwood Plantation: A Documentation of the Gardens." M.L.A. thesis, Louisiana State University School of Landscape Architecture, 1994.

Thomas Butler Papers. LLMVC.

Carter, Edward C., II, John C. Van Horne, and Charles E. Brownell, eds. *Latrobe's View of America, 1795–1820.* New Haven, 1985.

"Diary of My Uncle Gabriel Aime." Photocopy of typescript "given by my sister Nathalie, January 19, 1896," to Alcée Fortier, in author's possession.

Diderot, Denis. *Recueil de planches, sur les sciences, les arts libéraux, et les arts mécaniques, avec leur explication.* New York, 1969.

Diderot Encyclopedia: The Complete Illustrations, 1762–1777. Vol. I of 5 vols. New York, 1978.

Downing, Andrew Jackson. *The Horticulturist.* Albany, N.Y., 1846–52.

———. *A Treatise on the Theory and Practice of Landscape Gardening Adapted to North America.* 1841; rpr. Little Compton, R.I., 1981.

Drawings of the New Orleans Notarial Archives, 1808–1880s. New Orleans City Hall.

Farnsworth, Jean M., and Ann M. Masson, eds. *The Architecture of Colonial Louisiana: Collected Essays of Samuel Wilson, Jr., F.A.I.A.* Lafayette, La., 1987.

Faulkner, William. *Mosquitoes.* New York, 1927.

Files of Shadows-on-the-Teche, New Iberia, La.

Flint, Timothy. *Recollections of the Last Ten Years in the Valley of the Mississippi.* 1826; rpr. Carbondale, Ill., 1968.

Grandfort, Marie Fontenay de. *The New World.* Translated by E. C. Wharton. New Orleans, 1855.

Griswold, Mac, and Eleanor Weller. *The Golden Age of American Gardens: Proud Owners, Private Estates, 1890–1940.* New York, 1991.

Ingraham, Joseph Holt. *Travels in the Southwest by a Yankee.* Vol. I of 2 vols. 1835; rpr. Ann Arbor, Mich., 1966.

Jackson, John Brinckerhoff. *The Necessity for Ruins and Other Topics.* Amherst, Mass., 1980.

Kane, Harnett. *Plantation Parade.* New York, 1945.

King, Edward. "Old and New Louisiana." *Scribner's Monthly Magazine,* November, 1873, p. 10.

Kniffen, Fred B. *Louisiana: Its Land and People.* Baton Rouge, 1968.

———. "The Lower Mississippi Valley: European Settlement, Utilization, and Modification." In *Cultural Diffusion and Landscapes,* edited by H. Jesse Walker and Randall A. Detro. Baton Rouge, 1990.

Lawrence, Elizabeth. *A Southern Garden.* 1942; rpr. Chapel Hill, N.C., 1991.

Leeper, Robert. "Sugar Cane, Orange Blossoms, and Ostriches: A Remembrance, Interpretation, and Proposal for the Valcour Aime Plantation." B.L.A. thesis, LSU School of Landscape Architecture, 1991.

Lelièvre, J. F. *Nouveau Jardinier de la Louisiane, contenant les instructions necessaires aux personnes qui s'occupent de jardinage.* New Orleans, 1838.

"The Letters of Baron Joseph X. Pontalba to His Wife, 1796." Translated by Henri Delville de Sinclair. Survey of Federal Archives in Louisiana, WPA. Typescript in Louisiana State Museum Library, New Orleans.

The Letters of Marie-Madeleine Hachard, Ursuline of New Orleans, 1727–1728. Translated by Myldred Masson Costa. New Orleans, 1974.

Levasseur, A. "Lafayette's Visit to Baton Rouge, . . . from . . . *Lafayette in America, . . . 1829.*" Translated by R. W. Colomb. *Louisiana Historical Quarterly,* XIV (1931), 178–79.

Longworth, Maria [Thoeraese Yelverton]. *Teresina in America.* London, 1875.

Mackay, Alexander. *The Western World; or, Travels in the United States in 1846–47.* London, 1849.

Martin, R. P., Jr. "The Plantation Mansion and Estate of Valcour Aime." Photocopy in author's possession.

Miller, Henry. *The Air-Conditioned Nightmare.* New York, 1945.

Moore, Diane. *Live Oak Gardens: A Place of Peace and Beauty.* Lafayette, La., 1991.

Murray, Amelia. *Letters from the United States, Cuba, and Canada.* New York, 1856.

Olmsted, Frederick Law. *The Cotton Kingdom.* 1861; rpr. Indianapolis, 1971.

———. *A Journey in the Back Country.* 1860; rpr. New York, 1970.

———. *A Journey in the Seaboard Slave States, with Remarks on Their Economy.* New York, 1856.

Paret, Joseph. "Mon journal d'Amérique." Translated by Robert Landry. In process.

Perilloux, Kathleen Mills. "Evolution of the Site of Afton Villa." M.L.A. thesis, LSU School of Landscape Architecture, 1990.

Pitot, James. *Observations on the Colony of Louisiana from 1796 to 1802.* Translated by Henry C. Pitot. Baton Rouge, 1979.

Plantation Diary of the Late Mr. Valcour Aime. New Orleans, 1878.

"Plantation Diary of the Late Mr. Valcour Aime." Translated by Works Progress Administration, 1932. Microfiche in LSU Libraries.

Platt, Charles A. *Italian Gardens.* 1894; rpr. Portland, Oreg., 1993.

Reps, John W. *Cities of the Mississippi: Nineteenth-Century Images of Urban Development.* Columbia, Mo., 1994.

Ripley, Eliza. *Social Life in Old New Orleans, Being Recollections of My Girlhood.* New York, 1912.

Tankard, Judith B. *The Gardens of Ellen Biddle Shipman.* Sagaponack, N.Y., 1996.

Toledano, Roulhac B. "Louisiana's Golden Age: Valcour Aime in St. James Parish." *Louisiana History,* X (1969), 211–24.

Martha Turnbull Garden Diary, 1836–1895. Manuscript in Collection of Friends of Oakley, Oakley plantation, St. Francisville, La.

Weeks Family Papers. LLMVC.

Wilson, Samuel, Jr. *The Vieux Carre Historic District Demonstration Study: The Vieux Carre, New Orleans—Its Plan, Its Growth, Its Architecture.* New Orleans, 1968.

———, ed. *Southern Travels: Journal of John H. B. Latrobe.* New Orleans, 1986.

Index